Credits

Executive Editor
Jody Lefevere

Project Editor
Lynn Northrup

Technical Editor
Namir Shammas

Editorial Director
Robyn Siesky

Business Manager
Amy Knies

Senior Marketing Manager
Sandy Smith

Vice President and Executive Group Publisher
Richard Swadley

Vice President and Executive Publisher
Barry Pruett

Project Coordinator
Lynsey Stanford

Graphics and Production Specialists
Joyce Haughey
Andrea Hornberger
Jennifer Mayberry
Heather Pope

Quality Control Technicians
Melanie Hoffman
Lauren Mandelbaum
Susan Moritz

Proofreader
Mildred Rosenzweig

Indexer
Potomac Indexing, LLC

Screen Artist
Jill A. Proll

About the Author

Paul McFedries is a technical writer who has been authoring computer books since 1991. He has more than 60 books to his credit, which together have sold more than three million copies worldwide. These books include the Wiley titles *Teach Yourself VISUALLY Excel 2010*, *Teach Yourself VISUALLY Microsoft Office 2008 for Mac*, *Excel 2010 Visual Quick Tips*, and *Excel 2010 PivotTable and PivotCharts Visual Blueprint*. Paul also runs Word Spy, a Web site dedicated to tracking new words and phrases (see www.wordspy.com). Please visit Paul's personal Web site at www.mcfedries.com.

Author's Acknowledgments

The book you hold in your hands is not only an excellent learning tool, but it is truly beautiful, as well. I am happy to have supplied the text that you will read, but the gorgeous layout comes from Wiley's crack team of designers and screen artists. The layout of the tasks, the accuracy of the spelling and grammar, and the veracity of the information are all the result of hard work performed by project editor Lynn Northrup and technical editor Namir Shammas. Thanks to both of you for your excellent work. My thanks, as well, to executive editor Jody Lefevere for asking me to write this book.

How to Use This Book

Who This Book Is For

This book is for the reader who has never used this particular technology or software application. It is also for readers who want to expand their knowledge.

The Conventions in This Book

❶ Steps

This book uses a step-by-step format to guide you easily through each task. Numbered steps are actions you must do; bulleted steps clarify a point, step, or optional feature; and indented steps give you the result.

❷ Notes

Notes give additional information — special conditions that may occur during an operation, a situation that you want to avoid, or a cross reference to a related area of the book.

❸ Icons and Buttons

Icons and buttons show you exactly what you need to click to perform a step.

❹ Simplify It

Simplify It sections offer additional information, including warnings and shortcuts.

❺ Bold

Bold type shows command names, options, and text or numbers you must type.

❻ Italics

Italic type introduces and defines a new term.

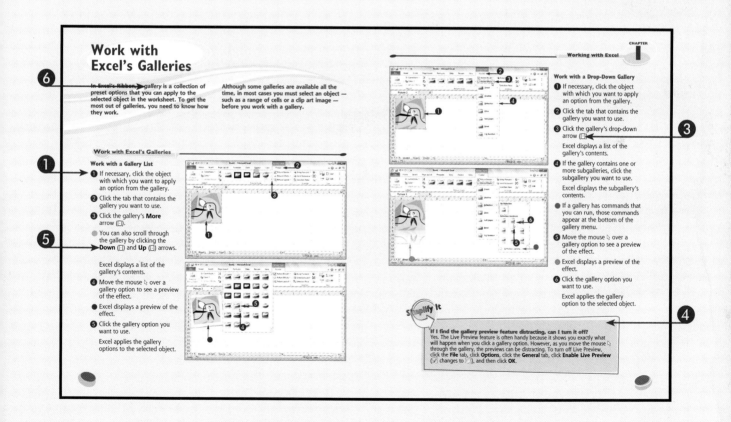

Table of Contents

3

Working with Excel Ranges

	A	Produ
1	**Category Name**	Produ
2	Beverages	Chai
3	Beverages	Chang
4	Beverages	Chartre
5	Beverages	Côte de
6	Beverages	Ipoh Co
7	Beverages	Lakkali
8	Beverages	Laughir
9	Beverages	Outbac
10	Beverages	Rhönbr
11	Beverages	Sasqua
12	Beverages	Steeley
13		see
14		Chef Ar

Sheet1 / Sheet2 / Shee

Ready

4

Working with Range Names

Create Names from Selection

Create names from values in the:

☑ Top row

☐ Left column

☐ Bottom row

☐ Right column

[OK] [Cancel]

Table of Contents

5

Formatting Excel Ranges

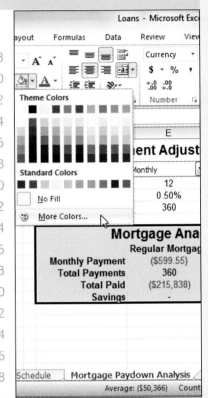

6

Building Formulas and Functions

7

Manipulating Excel Worksheets

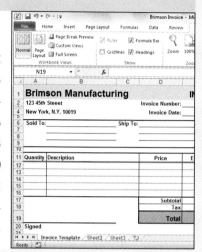

8

Dealing with Excel Workbooks

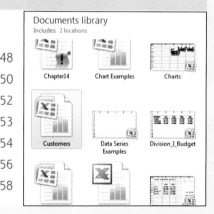

9

Formatting Excel Workbooks

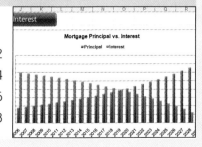

Table of Contents

10

Analyzing Excel Data

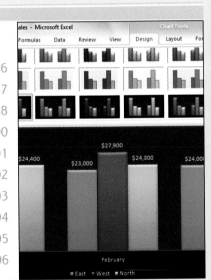

11

Visualizing Data with Excel Charts

12

Formatting Excel Charts

13

Collaborating with Other People

Chapter 1

Working with Excel

You use Microsoft Excel to create *spreadsheets*, which are documents that enable you to manipulate numbers and formulas to quickly create powerful mathematical, financial, and statistical models. In this chapter you learn about Excel and you find out the kinds of tasks you can perform with Excel. You also learn how to start the program, and you take a tour of the program's major features. This chapter also shows you how to work with Excel Ribbon and the Ribbon's galleries, how to customize the Ribbon and the Quick Access Toolbar, how to work with smart tags, and how to customize the view and other aspects of the program.

Getting to Know Excel

Working with Excel involves two basic tasks: building a spreadsheet and then manipulating the data on the spreadsheet. Building a spreadsheet involves adding data, formulas, and functions. Manipulating data involves calculating totals, working with series, creating tables for your data, and visualizing data in charts.

This section just gives you an overview of these tasks. You learn about each task in greater detail as you work through the book.

Build a Spreadsheet

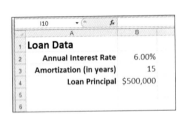

Add Data

You can insert text, numbers, and other characters into any cell in the spreadsheet. Click the cell that you want to work with and then type your data in the Formula bar. This is the large text box above the column letters. Your typing appears in the cell that you selected. When you are done, press Enter. To edit existing cell data, click the cell and then edit the text in the Formula bar.

Add a Formula

A *formula* is a collection of numbers, cell addresses, and mathematical operators that performs a calculation. In Excel, you enter a formula in a cell by typing an equal sign (**=**) and then the formula text. For example, the formula =B1-B2 subtracts the value in cell B2 from the value in cell B1.

Add a Function

A *function* is a predefined formula that performs a specific task. For example, the AVERAGE function calculates the average of a list of numbers, and the PMT function calculates a loan or mortgage payment. You can use functions on their own, preceded by **=**, or as part of a larger formula. Click **Insert Function** (*fx*) to see a list of the available functions.

Manipulate Data

Calculate Totals Quickly

If you just need a quick sum of a list of numbers, click a cell below the numbers and then click the **Sum** button (Σ), which is available in the Home tab of Excel's Ribbon. In Excel, you can also select the cells that you want to sum, and their total appears in the status bar.

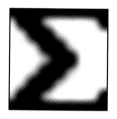

Fill a Series

Excel enables you to save time by completing a series of values automatically. For example, if you need to enter the numbers 1 to 100 in consecutive cells, you can enter just the first few numbers, select the cells, and then click and drag the lower right corner to fill in the rest of the numbers. Most programs also fill in dates, as well as the names for weekdays and months.

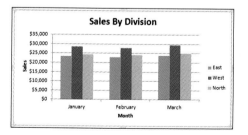

Manage Tables

The row-and-column format of a spreadsheet makes the program suitable for simple databases called *tables*. Each column becomes a field in the table, and each row is a record. You can sort the records, filter the records to show only certain values, and add subtotals.

Add a Chart

A *chart* is a graphic representation of spreadsheet data. As the data in the spreadsheet changes, the chart also changes to reflect the new numbers. Excel offers a wide variety of charts, including bar charts, line charts, and pie charts.

Start Excel

Before you can perform tasks such as adding data and building formulas, you must first start Excel. This brings the Excel window onto the Windows desktop, and you can then begin using the program. This task and the rest of the book assume that you have already installed Excel 2010 on your computer.

When you have finished your work with Excel, you should shut down the program. This reduces clutter on the desktop and in the taskbar, and it also conserves memory and other system resources.

Start Excel

① Click **Start**.

The Start menu appears.

② Click **All Programs**.

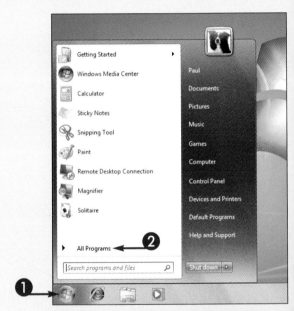

The App Programs menu appears.

③ Click **Microsoft Office**.

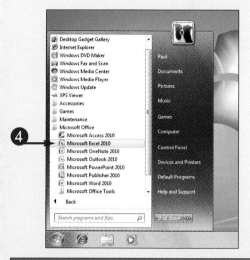

The Microsoft Office menu appears.

④ Click **Microsoft Excel 2010**.

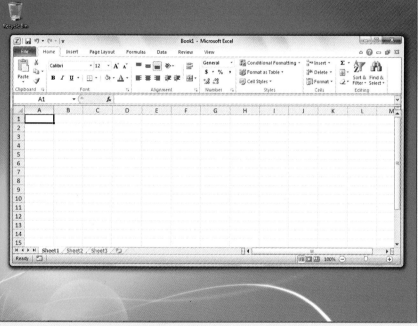

The Microsoft Excel window appears on the desktop.

Note: *When you are finished with Excel, close the program by clicking the* ***File*** *tab and then clicking* ***Exit***.

Are there faster methods I can use to start Excel?
Yes. After you have used Excel a few times, it should appear on the main Start menu in the list of your most-used programs. If so, you can click that icon to start the program. You can also force the Excel icon onto the Start menu by following Steps **1** to **3**, right-clicking the **Microsoft Excel 2010** icon, and then clicking **Pin to Start Menu**. If you are using Windows 7, you can also click **Pin to Taskbar** to add the Excel icon to the taskbar.

Tour the Excel Window

To get up to speed quickly with Excel, it helps to understand the various elements of the Excel window. These include standard window elements such as the title bar and status bar, as well as Office-specific elements such as the Ribbon and the File tab.

Title Bar

The title bar displays the name of the current workbook.

Quick Access Toolbar

This area gives you one-click access to a few often-used features. To learn how to customize this toolbar, see "Customize the Quick Access Toolbar."

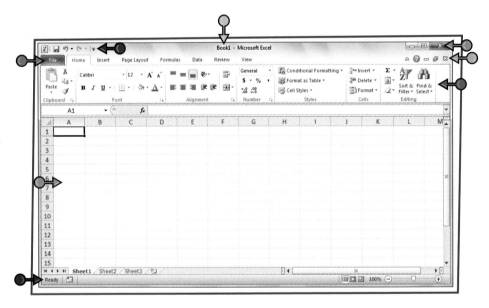

Ribbon

This area gives you access to all of Excel's commands, options, and features. To learn how to use this element, see "Work with Excel's Ribbon."

Excel Window Controls

You use these controls to minimize, maximize, restore, and close Excel's application window.

Workbook Window Controls

You use these controls to minimize, maximize, restore, and close the current workbook window.

File Tab

Click this tab to access file-related commands, such as Save and Open.

Worksheet

This area displays the current worksheet, and it is where you will do most of your Excel work.

Status Bar

This area displays messages about Excel's current status, the results of certain operations, and other information.

Work with Excel's Ribbon

You use Excel's Ribbon element to access all of the program's features and commands. The *Ribbon* is the horizontal strip that runs across the top of the Excel window, just below the title bar. The Ribbon is organized into various tabs, such as File, Home, and Insert, and each tab contains related controls, which usually include buttons, lists, and check boxes. There is no menu bar in Excel, so you do not use pull-down menus to access commands.

Work with Excel's Ribbon

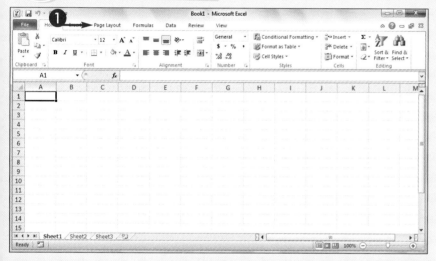

1 Click the tab that contains the Excel feature you want to work with.

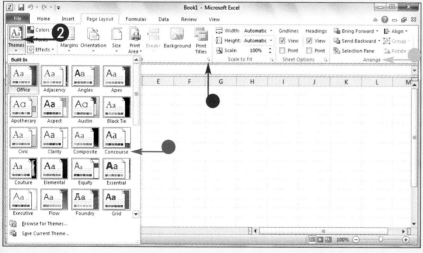

Excel displays the controls in the tab.

● Each tab is organized into groups of related controls, and the group names appear here.

● In many groups you can click the dialog box launcher button (▢) to display a dialog box that contains group settings.

2 Click the control for the feature.

● If the control displays a list of options, click the option you want.

Excel runs the command or sets the option.

9

Work with Excel's Galleries

In Excel's Ribbon, a *gallery* is a collection of preset options that you can apply to the selected object in the worksheet. To get the most out of galleries, you need to know how they work.

Although some galleries are available all the time, in most cases you must select an object — such as a range of cells or a clip art image — before you work with a gallery.

Work with Excel's Galleries

Work with a Gallery List

1 If necessary, click the object with which you want to apply an option from the gallery.

2 Click the tab that contains the gallery you want to use.

3 Click the gallery's **More** arrow (⊡).

● You can also scroll through the gallery by clicking the **Down** (⊡) and **Up** (⊡) arrows.

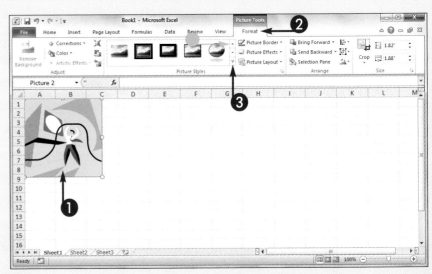

Excel displays a list of the gallery's contents.

4 Move the mouse ☇ over a gallery option to see a preview of the effect.

● Excel displays a preview of the effect.

5 Click the gallery option you want to use.

Excel applies the gallery options to the selected object.

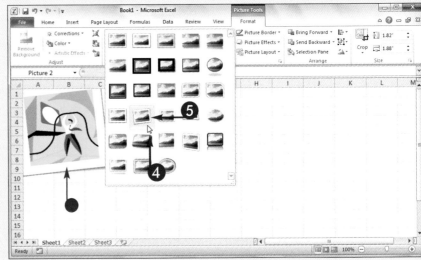

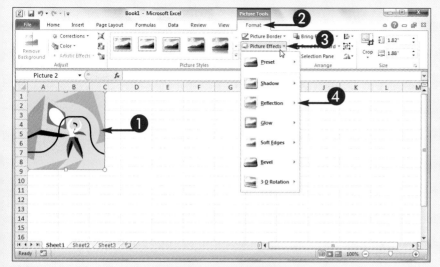

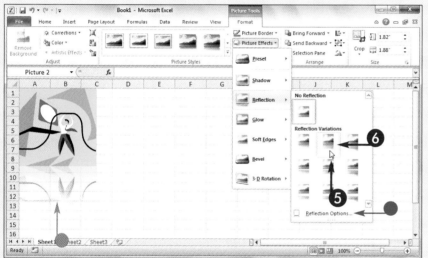

Work with a Drop-Down Gallery

1 If necessary, click the object with which you want to apply an option from the gallery.

2 Click the tab that contains the gallery you want to use.

3 Click the gallery's drop-down arrow (⊡).

Excel displays a list of the gallery's contents.

4 If the gallery contains one or more subgalleries, click the subgallery you want to use.

Excel displays the subgallery's contents.

● If a gallery has commands that you can run, those commands appear at the bottom of the gallery menu.

5 Move the mouse ⫢ over a gallery option to see a preview of the effect.

● Excel displays a preview of the effect.

6 Click the gallery option you want to use.

Excel applies the gallery option to the selected object.

If I find the gallery preview feature distracting, can I turn it off?
Yes. The Live Preview feature is often handy because it shows you exactly what will happen when you click a gallery option. However, as you move the mouse ⫢ through the gallery, the previews can be distracting. To turn off Live Preview, click the **File** tab, click **Options**, click the **General** tab, click **Enable Live Preview** (☑ changes to ☐), and then click **OK**.

Customize the Quick Access Toolbar

You can make Excel easier to use by customizing the Quick Access Toolbar to include the Excel commands you use most often. You run Quick Access Toolbar buttons with a single click, so adding your favorite commands saves time. By default, the Quick Access Toolbar contains three buttons: Save, Undo, and Redo, but you can add any of Excel's hundreds of commands.

Since there is only so much room for the Quick Access Toolbar in Excel's menu bar, consider moving the Quick Access Toolbar below the Ribbon to gain more space for your custom commands.

Customize the Quick Access Toolbar

1 Click the **Customize Quick Access Toolbar** button (⊡).

● If you see the command you want, click it and skip the rest of the steps in this section.

2 Click **More Commands**.

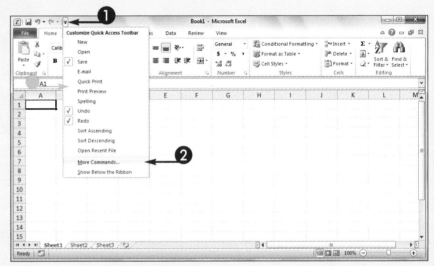

The Excel Options dialog box appears.

● Excel automatically displays the Quick Access Toolbar tab.

3 Click the **Choose commands from** ⊡.

4 Click the command category you want to use.

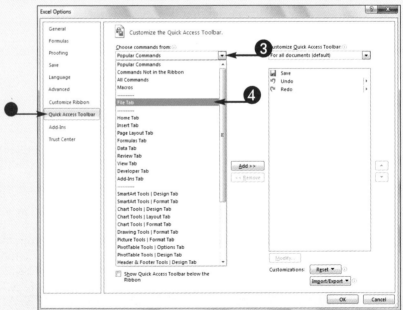

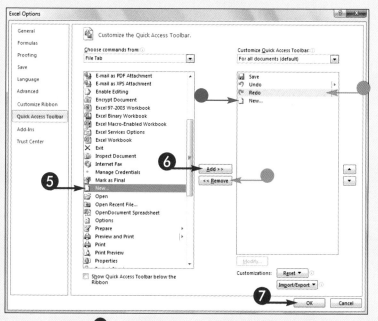

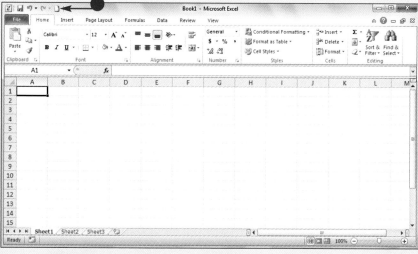

5 Click the command you want to add.

6 Click **Add**.

● Excel adds the command.

● To remove a command, click it and then click **Remove**.

7 Click **OK**.

● Excel adds a button for the command to the Quick Access Toolbar.

Can I get more room on the Quick Access Toolbar to show more buttons?
Yes, you can increase the space available to the Quick Access Toolbar by moving it below the Ribbon. This gives the toolbar the full width of the Excel window, so you can add many more buttons. Click the **Customize Quick Access Toolbar** button (▾) and then click **Show Below the Ribbon**.

Is there a faster way to add buttons to the Quick Access Toolbar?
Yes. If the command you want to add appears on the Ribbon, you can add a button for the command directly from the Ribbon. Click the Ribbon tab that contains the command, right-click the command, and then click **Add to Quick Access Toolbar**. Excel inserts a button for the command on the Quick Access Toolbar.

Customize the Ribbon

You can improve your Excel productivity by customizing the Ribbon with extra commands that you use frequently. The default Ribbon contains eight tabs, and each of those tabs contains dozens of commands in the form of buttons, galleries, lists, and other controls. However, Excel has many other commands

available, and you may wish to add one or more of these other commands if you use any of them frequently.

To add a new command to the Ribbon, you must first create a new tab or a new group within an existing tab, and then add the command to the new tab or group.

Customize the Ribbon

Display the Customize Ribbon Tab

1. Right-click any part of the Ribbon.

2. Click **Customize the Ribbon**.

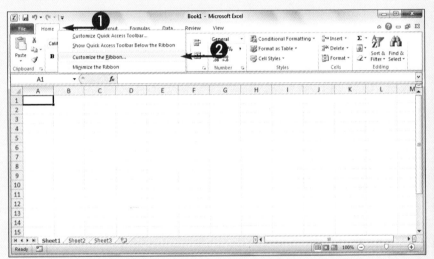

Add a New Tab or Group

The Excel Options dialog box appears.

● Excel automatically displays the Customize Ribbon tab.

1. Click the tab you want to customize.

● You can also click **New Tab** to create a custom tab.

2. Click **New Group**.

● Excel adds the group.

3. Click **Rename**.

4. Type a name for the group.

5. Click **OK**.

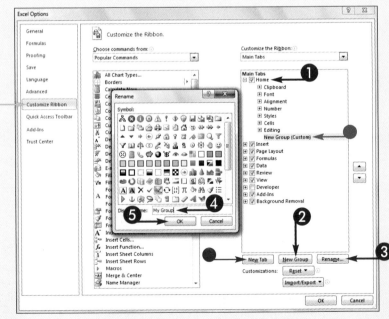

14

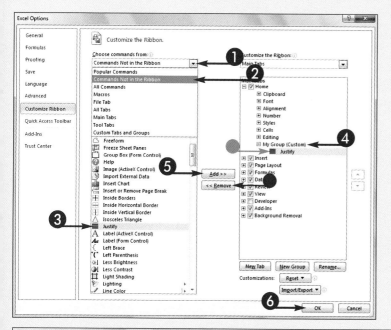

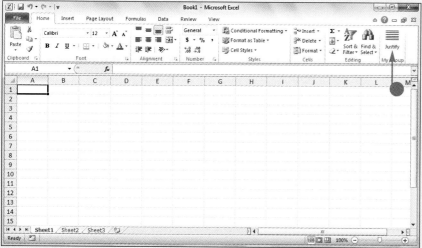

Add a Command

① Click the **Choose commands from** ☐.

② Click the command category you want to use.

③ Click the command you want to add.

④ Click the custom group or tab you want to use.

⑤ Click **Add**.

⬤ Excel adds the command.

⬤ To remove a custom command, click it and then click **Remove**.

⑥ Click **OK**.

⬤ Excel adds the new group and command to the Ribbon.

Simplify It

Can I customize the tabs that appear only when I select an Excel object?
Yes. Excel calls these *tool tabs*, and you can add custom groups and commands to any tool tab. Right-click any part of the Ribbon and then click **Customize the Ribbon** to display the Excel Options dialog box with the Customize Ribbon tab displayed. Click the **Customize the Ribbon** ☐ and then click **Tool Tabs**. Click the tab you want and then follow the steps in this section to customize it.

How do I restore the Ribbon to its default configuration?
Right-click any part of the Ribbon and then click **Customize the Ribbon** to display the Excel Options dialog box with the Customize Ribbon tab displayed. To restore a tab, click the tab, click **Restore Defaults**, and then click **Restore only selected Ribbon tab**. To remove all customizations, click **Restore Defaults** and then click **Restore all Ribbon tabs and Quick Access Toolbar customizations**.

Work with Smart Tags

You can make your Excel work faster and easier by taking advantage of smart tags. A *smart tag* is a special icon that appears when you perform certain Excel tasks, such as pasting data and using the AutoFill feature. Clicking the smart tag displays a list of options that enable you to control or modify the task you just performed. Some smart tags appear automatically in response to certain conditions. For example, if Excel detects an inconsistent formula, it displays a smart tag to let you know.

Work with Smart Tags

1 Perform an action that displays a smart tag, such as copying and pasting a cell as shown here.

● The smart tag appears.

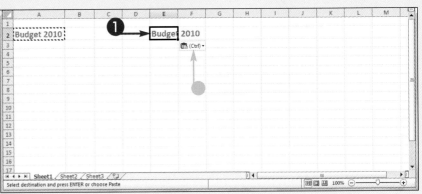

2 Click the smart tag.

● The smart tag displays a list of its options.

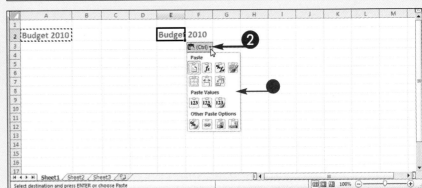

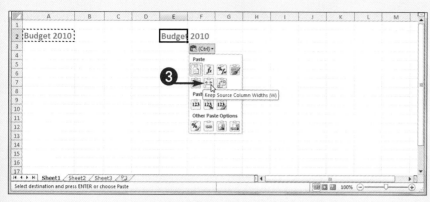

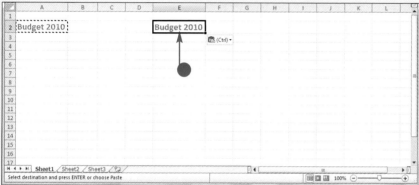

❸ Click the option you want to apply.

● Excel applies the option to the task you performed in Step **1**.

Are there other types of smart tags I can use?
Yes, Excel offers a few other smart tag types. For
example, a Date smart tag recognizes a worksheet
date and offers options such as scheduling a meeting
on that date. To turn on these extra smart tags, click
File, click **Options**, click **Proofing**, click **AutoCorrect
Options**, and then click the **Smart Tags** tab. Click the
Label data with smart tags check box (☐ changes
to ☑), and then click the check box beside each
smart tag in the **Recognizers** list (☐ changes to ☑).
Click **OK**.

Change the View

You can adjust the Excel window to suit what you are currently working on by changing the view to match your current task. Excel offers three different views: Page Layout, which displays worksheets as they would appear if

you printed them out; Page Break Preview, which displays the page breaks as blue lines, as described in the first Tip on the next page; and Normal, which is useful for building and editing worksheets.

Change the View

Switch to Page Layout View

1 Click the **View** tab.

2 Click **Page Layout**.

● You can also click the **Page Layout** button (▣).

● Excel switches to Page Layout view.

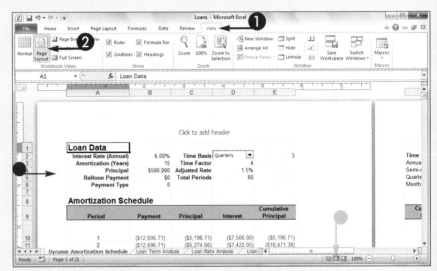

Switch to Page Break Preview

1 Click the **View** tab.

2 Click **Page Break Preview**.

● You can also click the **Page Break Preview** button (▣).

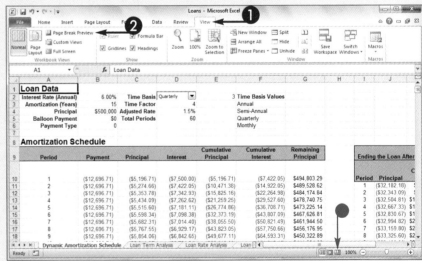

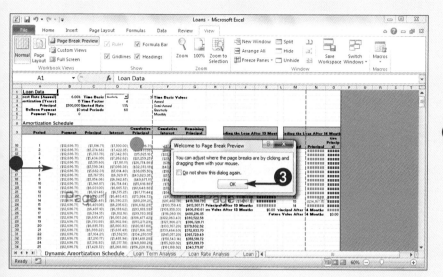

- The Welcome to Page Break Preview dialog box appears.

- Excel switches to Page Break Preview.

3 Click **OK**.

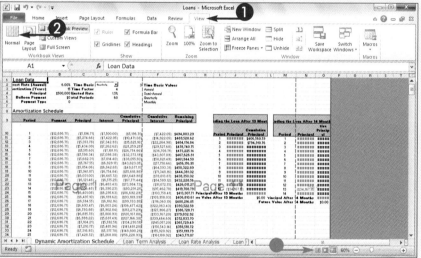

Switch to Normal View

1 Click the **View** tab.

2 Click **Normal**.

- You can also click the **Normal** button (▦).

  Excel switches to Normal view.

Simplify It

What does Page Break Preview do?

In Excel, a *page break* is a position within a worksheet where a new page begins when you print the worksheet. When you switch to Page Break Preview, Excel displays the page breaks as blue lines. If a page break occurs in a bad position — for example, the page break includes the headings from a range, but not the cells below the headings — you can use your mouse ⌖ to click and drag the page breaks to new positions.

What does Full Screen view do?

Full Screen view is useful when you want to see the maximum amount of a worksheet on the screen. Full Screen view removes many of the Excel window features, including the File button, Ribbon, Quick Access Toolbar, Formula bar, and status bar. To return to the Normal view, press `Esc`, or click the **Restore Down** button (▣).

Configure Excel Options

You can customize Excel and set up the program to suit the way you work by configuring the Excel options. You use these options to set your Excel preferences in a number of program categories, including formulas, proofing, and saving.

To use these options, you must know how to display the Excel Options dialog box. These options are dialog box controls such as check boxes, option buttons, and lists that enable you to configure many aspects of Excel.

Configure Excel Options

1 Click the **File** tab.

2 Click **Options**.

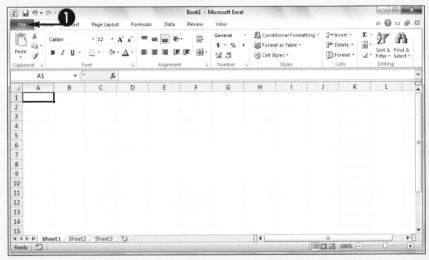

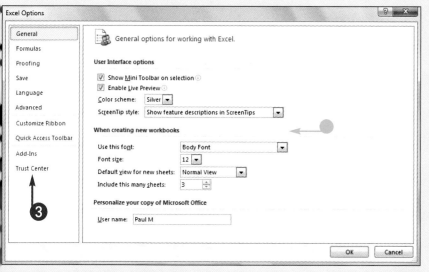

The Excel Options dialog box appears.

3 Click a tab on the left side of the dialog box to choose the configuration category you want to work with.

● The controls that appear on the right side of the dialog box change according to the tab you select.

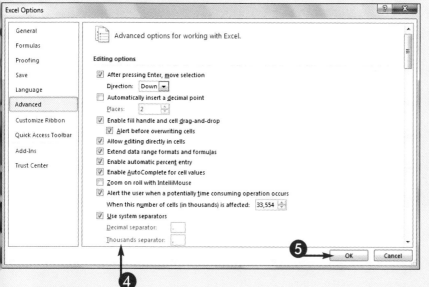

4 Use the controls on the right side of the dialog box to configure the options you want to change.

5 Click **OK**.

Excel puts the new options into effect.

Simplify It

Are there faster methods I can use to open the Excel Options dialog box?
Yes. Some features of the Excel interface offer shortcut methods that get you to the Excel Options dialog box faster. For example, right-click the Ribbon and then click **Customize Ribbon** to open the Excel Options dialog box with the Customize Ribbon tab displayed. From the keyboard, you can open the Excel Options dialog box by pressing Alt + F and then pressing I.

How do I know what each option does?
Excel offers pop-up descriptions of some — but, unfortunately, not all — of the options. If you see a small *i* with a circle around it to the right of the option name, it means pop-up help is available for that option. Hover the mouse over the option and Excel displays a pop-up description of the option after a second or two.

Chapter 2

Entering and Editing Excel Data

Are you ready to start using Excel to build a spreadsheet? To create a spreadsheet in Excel, you must understand the layout of an Excel worksheet as well as the types of data that you can enter into a worksheet. You also must know how to enter data — including text, numbers, dates, times, and symbols — into the worksheet cells, and how to edit that data to fix typos, adjust information, and remove data you no longer need.

Learning the Layout of a Worksheet

In Excel, a spreadsheet file is called a *workbook*, and each workbook consists of one or more *worksheets*. These worksheets are where you do most of your work in Excel — including entering your data and formulas — so you need to know the layout of a typical worksheet.

Cell
A *cell* is a box in which you enter your spreadsheet data.

Column
A *column* is a vertical line of cells. Each column has a unique letter that identifies it. For example, the leftmost column is A, and the next column is B.

Row
A *row* is a horizontal line of cells. Each row has a unique number that identifies it. For example, the topmost row is 1, and the next row is 2.

Mouse Pointer
Use the Excel mouse ⊕ to select cells.

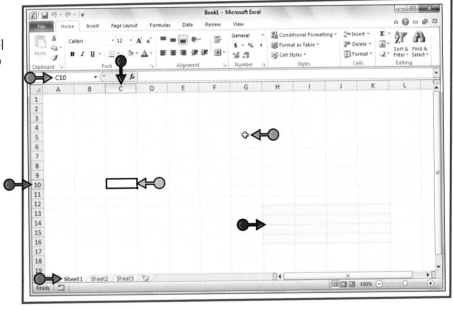

Cell Address
Each cell has its own *address*, which is determined by the letter and number of the intersecting column and row. For example, the cell at the intersection of column C and row 10 has the address C10.

Worksheet Tab
The worksheet tab displays the worksheet name. Most workbooks contain multiple worksheets, and you use the tabs to navigate between the worksheets.

Range
A *range* is a rectangular grouping of two or more cells. The range address is given by the address of the top left cell and the address of the bottom right cell. H12:K16 is an example of a range of cells, and it refers to all of the cells selected between column H, cell 12 and column K, cell 16.

Understanding the Types of Data You Can Use

To build a spreadsheet in Excel, it helps to understand the three main types of data that you can enter into a cell: text, numbers, and dates and times.

Text

Text entries can include any combination of letters, symbols, and numbers. You will mostly use text to describe the contents of your worksheets. This is very important because even a modest-sized spreadsheet can become a confusing jumble of numbers without some kind of text guidelines to keep things straight. Most text entries are usually labels such as *Sales* or *Territory* that make a worksheet easier to read. However, text entries can also be text/number combinations for items such as phone numbers and account codes.

	A	B	C
1	Category Name	Product Name	Quantity Per Unit
2	Beverages	Chai	10 boxes x 20 bags
3	Beverages	Chang	24 - 12 oz bottles
4	Beverages	Chartreuse verte	750 cc per bottle
5	Beverages	Côte de Blaye	12 - 75 cl bottles
6	Beverages	Ipoh Coffee	16 - 500 g tins
7	Beverages	Lakkalikööri	500 ml
8	Beverages	Laughing Lumberjack Lager	24 - 12 oz bottles
9	Beverages	Outback Lager	24 - 355 ml bottles
10	Beverages	Rhönbräu Klosterbier	24 - 0.5 l bottles
11	Beverages	Sasquatch Ale	24 - 12 oz bottles
12	Beverages	Steeleye Stout	24 - 12 oz bottles
13	Condiments	Aniseed Syrup	12 - 550 ml bottles
14	Condiments	Chef Anton's Cajun Seasoning	48 - 6 oz jars
15	Condiments	Genen Shouyu	24 - 250 ml bottles

Numbers

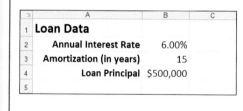

	A	B	C
1	Loan Data		
2	Annual Interest Rate	6.00%	
3	Amortization (in years)	15	
4	Loan Principal	$500,000	
5			

Numbers are the most common type of Excel data. The numbers you enter into a cell can be dollar values, weights, interest rates, temperatures, or any other numerical quantity. In most cases you just type the number that you want to appear in the cell. However, you can also precede a number with a dollar sign ($) or other currency symbol to indicate a monetary value, or follow a number with a percent sign (%) to indicate a percentage value.

Dates and Times

Date entries appear in spreadsheets that include dated data, such as invoices and sales. You can either type out the full date — such as August 23, 2010 — or use either the forward slash (/) or the hyphen (-) as a date separator — such as 8/23/2010 or 8-23-2010. Note that the order you enter the date values depends on your regional settings. For example, in the United States the format is month/day/year. For time values, you use a colon (:) as a time separator, followed by either AM or PM — such as 9:15 AM.

	A	B	C	D	E	F
8	Date	Work Start Time	Lunch Start Time	Lunch End Time	Work End Time	Total Hours Worked
9	Monday Sep 6, 2010	9:00 AM	12:00 PM	1:00 PM	5:00 PM	7:00
10	Tuesday Sep 7, 2010	8:00 AM	12:30 PM	1:45 PM	5:00 PM	7:45
11	Wednesday Sep 8, 2010	9:00 AM	12:15 PM	1:15 PM	5:30 PM	7:30
12	Thursday Sep 9, 2010	8:45 AM	1:00 PM	2:00 PM	5:00 PM	7:15
13	Friday Sep 10, 2010	9:00 AM	12:45 PM	1:45 PM	5:00 PM	7:00

Enter Text into a Cell

Your first step when building a spreadsheet is usually to enter the text data that defines the spreadsheet's labels or headings. This is particularly important if other people will be reading or editing the spreadsheet, because the labels and headings help people make sense of the data and help them understand the purpose of the spreadsheet.

Most labels appear in the cell to the right or above where the data will appear, while most headings appear at the top of a column of data or to the left of a row of data.

Enter Text into a Cell

① Click the cell in which you want to enter the text.

● Excel marks the current cell by surrounding it with a thick, black border.

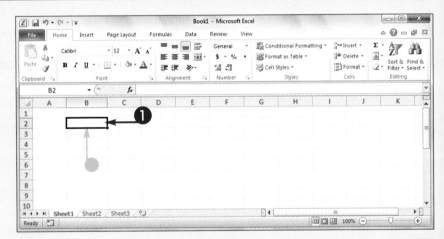

② Start typing your text.

● Excel opens the cell for editing and displays the text as you type.

● Your typing also appears in the Formula bar.

Note: *Rather than typing the text directly into the cell, you can also type the text into the Formula bar.*

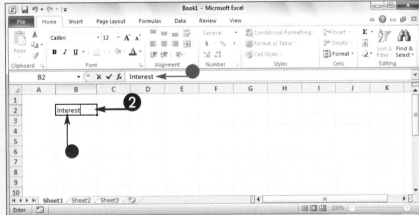

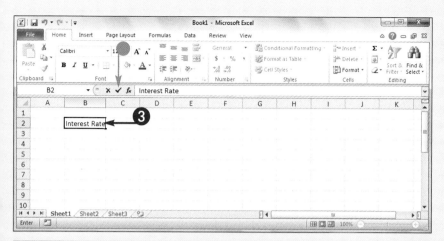

❸ When your text entry is complete, press Enter.

● If you do not want Excel to move the selection, click **Enter** (☑) or press Ctrl + Enter instead.

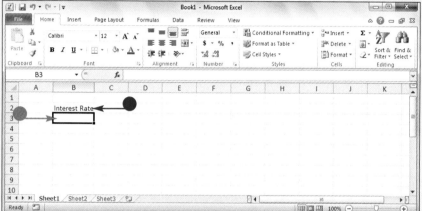

● Excel closes the cell for editing.

● If you pressed Enter, Excel moves the selection to the cell below.

When I press Enter, the selection moves to the next cell down. Can I make the selection move to the right instead?
Yes. When you have finished adding the data to the cell, press →. This tells Excel to close the current cell for editing and move the selection to the next cell on the right. If you prefer to move left instead, press ←; if you prefer to move up, press ↑.

When I start typing text into a cell, why does Excel sometimes display the text from another cell?
This is part of an Excel feature called AutoComplete. If the letters you type at the start of a cell match the contents of another cell in the worksheet, Excel fills in the full text from the other cell under the assumption that you are repeating the text in the new cell. If you want to use the text, click ☑ or press Enter; otherwise, just keep typing your text.

Enter a Number into a Cell

Excel is all about numbers, so most of your worksheets will include numeric values. Some worksheets store only numeric values, but most use numbers as the basis for one or more calculations, such as monthly loan payments, statistical analysis, or budget totals.

To get the most out of Excel, you need to know how to enter numeric values, including percentages and currency values.

Enter a Number into a Cell

1 Click the cell in which you want to enter the number.

● Excel marks the current cell by surrounding it with a thick, black border.

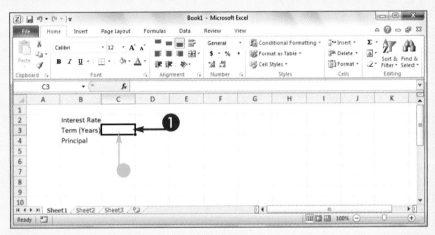

2 Start typing your number.

● Excel opens the cell for editing and displays the number as you type.

● Your typing also appears in the Formula bar.

Note: Rather than typing the number directly into the cell, you can also type the number into the Formula bar.

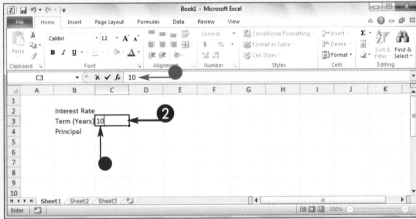

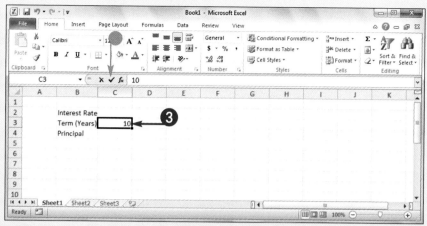

③ When your number is complete, press Enter.

● If you do not want Excel to move the selection, click **Enter** (☑) or press Ctrl + Enter instead.

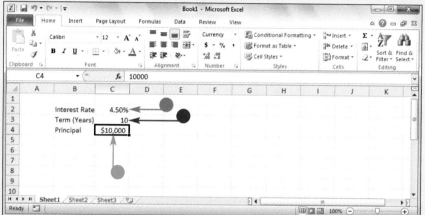

● Excel closes the cell for editing.

● To enter a percentage value, type the number followed by a percent sign (%).

● To enter a currency value, type the dollar sign ($) followed by the number.

Simplify It

Can I use symbols such as a comma, decimal point, or minus sign when I enter a numeric value?

Yes. If your numeric value is in the thousands, you can include the thousands separator (,) within the number. For example, if you enter **10000**, Excel displays the value as 10000; however, if you enter **10,000**, Excel displays the value as 10,000, which is easier to read. If your numeric value includes one or more decimals, you can include the decimal point (.) when you type the value. If your numeric value is negative, precede the value with a minus sign (–).

Is there a quick way to repeat a number rather than entering the entire number all over again?

Excel offers a few methods for doing this. The easiest method is to select the cell directly below the value you want to repeat and then press Ctrl + '. Excel adds the value to the cell. For another method, see "Fill a Range with the Same Data" in Chapter 3.

Enter a Date or Time into a Cell

Many Excel worksheets use dates either as part of the sheet data or for use in calculations, such as the number of days an invoice is overdue. Excel worksheets also often use times, such as recording when a transaction took place or calculating the total number of hours an employee has worked in a given period.

For these and similar uses, you need to know how to enter date and time values into a cell.

Enter a Date or Time into a Cell

Enter a Date

① Click the cell in which you want to enter the date.

● Excel marks the current cell by surrounding it with a thick, black border.

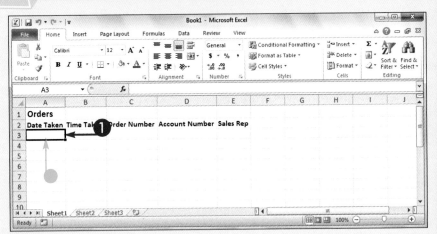

② Type the date.

> **Note:** The format you use depends on your location. In the United States, for example, you can use the month/day/year format — 8/23/2010. See the Tip on the next page.

③ When your date is complete, press Enter.

● If you do not want Excel to move the selection, click **Enter** (☑) or press Ctrl + Enter instead.

Excel closes the cell for editing.

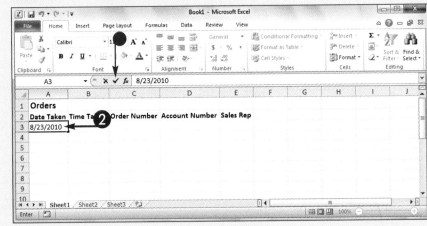

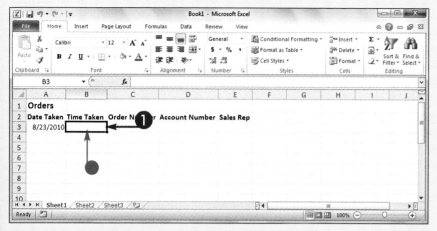

Enter a Time

1 Click the cell in which you want to enter the time.

● Excel marks the current cell by surrounding it with a thick, black border.

2 Type the time.

Note: The general format for entering a time is hour:minute:second AM/PM; for example, 3:15:00 PM. See the following Tip.

3 When your time is complete, press **Enter**.

● If you do not want Excel to move the selection, click **Enter** (☑) or press **Ctrl** + **Enter** instead.

Excel closes the cell for editing.

Simplify It

How can I tell which date and time formats my version of Excel accepts?
Follow these steps:

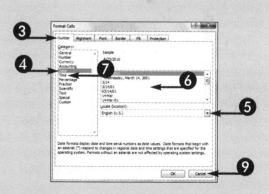

1 Click the **Home** tab.

2 Click the dialog box launcher button in the bottom right corner of the Number group.

3 Click the **Number** tab.

4 Click **Date**.

5 Click the **Locale (location)** drop-down arrow ⏷ and then click your location.

6 Examine the Type list to see the formats you can use to enter dates.

7 Click **Time**.

8 Examine the Type list to see the formats you can use to enter times.

9 Click **Cancel**.

Insert a Symbol

You can make your Excel worksheets more readable and more useful by inserting special symbols that are not available via your keyboard's standard keys. These special symbols include foreign characters such as ö and é, mathematical symbols such as ÷ and ∞, financial symbols such as ¢ and ¥, commercial symbols such as © and ®, and many more.

Insert a Symbol

1 Click the cell in which you want the symbol to appear.

2 Type the text that you want to appear before the symbol, if any.

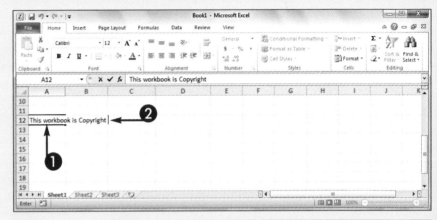

3 Click the **Insert** tab.

4 Click **Symbol**.

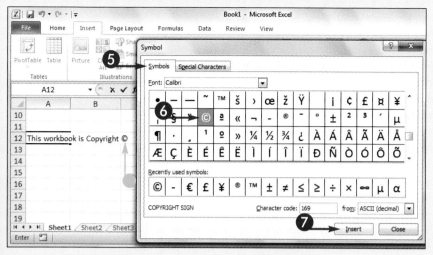

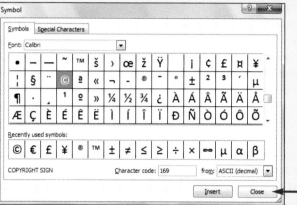

The Symbol dialog box appears.

⑤ Click the **Symbols** tab.

⑥ Click the symbol you want to insert.

Note: *Many other symbols are available in the Webdings and Wingdings fonts. To see these symbols, click the **Font** ⊡, and then click either **Webdings** or **Wingdings**.*

⑦ Click **Insert**.

● Excel inserts the symbol.

⑧ Repeat Steps **6** and **7** to insert any other symbols you require.

⑨ Click **Close**.

Are there keyboard shortcuts available for symbols I use frequently?
Yes, in many cases. In the Symbol dialog box, click ⊡ in the from list and select **ASCII (decimal)**. Click the symbol you want to insert and then examine the number in the Character code text box. This number tells you that you can enter the symbol via the keyboard by holding down Alt, pressing 0, and then typing the number. For example, you can enter the © symbol by pressing Alt + 0 1 6 9. Be sure to type all the numbers using your keyboard's numeric keypad.

Edit Cell Data

Once you enter text, a number, a date, or a time into a cell, that cell data is not set in stone. If the data you entered into a cell has changed or is incorrect, you can edit the data to the updated or correct value. You can edit cell data either directly in the cell or by using the Formula bar.

Edit Cell Data

① Click the cell in which you want to edit the text.

② Press **F2**.

You can also double-click the cell you want to edit.

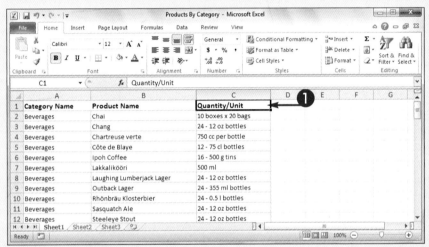

● Excel opens the cell for editing and moves the cursor to the end of the existing data.

● Excel displays Edit in the status bar.

● You can also click inside the Formula bar and edit the cell data there.

③ Make your changes to the cell data.

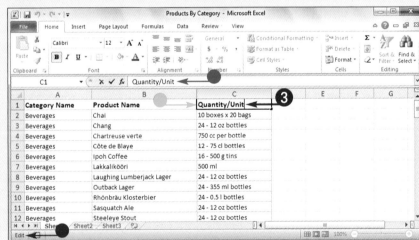

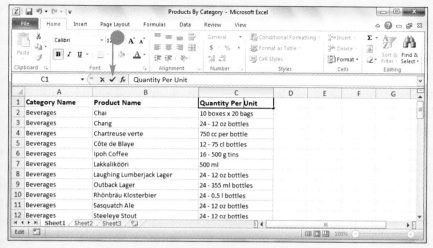

④ When you finish editing the data, press Enter.

● If you do not want Excel to move the selection, click **Enter** (☑) or press Ctrl + Enter instead.

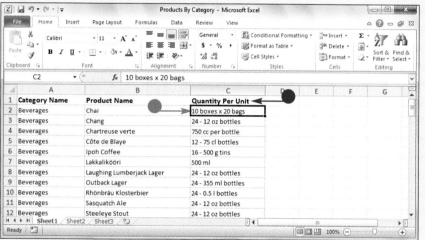

● Excel closes the cell for editing.

● If you pressed Enter, Excel moves the selection to the cell below.

Simplify It

Is there a faster way to open a cell for editing?

Yes. Move ⬚ over the cell you want to edit, and center ⬚ over the character where you want to start editing. Double-click the mouse. Excel opens the cell for editing and positions the cursor at the spot where you double-clicked.

I made a mistake when I edited a cell. Do I have to fix the text by hand?

Most likely not. If the cell edit was the last action you performed in Excel, press Ctrl + Z or click the **Undo** button (⟲) in the Quick Launch Toolbar. If you have performed other actions in the meantime, click the **Undo** ⬚ and then click the edit in the list that appears. Note, however, that doing this will also undo the other actions you performed after the edit.

Delete Data from a Cell

If your worksheet has a cell that contains data you no longer need, you can delete that data. This helps to reduce worksheet clutter and makes your worksheet easier to read. If you want to delete data from multiple cells, you must first select those cells; see "Select a Range" in Chapter 3. To delete cells and not just the data, see "Delete a Range" in Chapter 3.

Delete Data from a Cell

Delete Cell Data

① Select the cell that contains the data you want to delete.

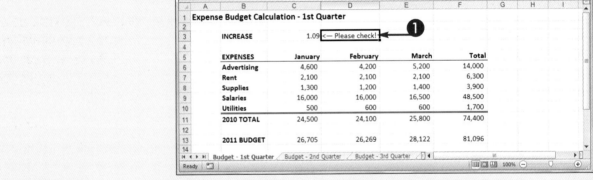

② Click the **Home** tab.

③ Click **Clear** (⬚).

④ Click **Clear Contents**.

Note: You can also delete cell data by pressing Delete.

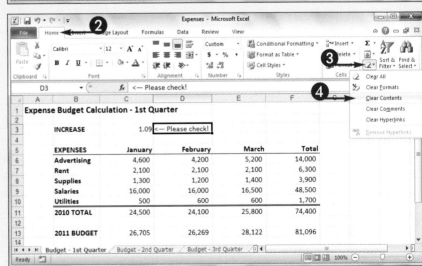

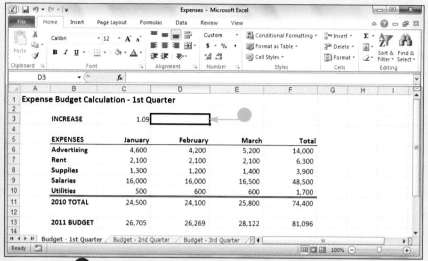

● Excel removes the cell data.

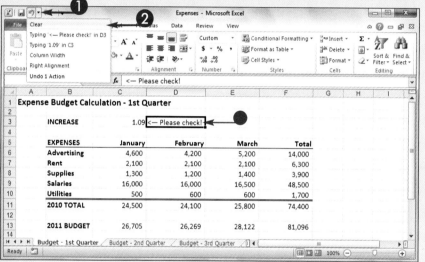

Undo Cell Data Deletion

❶ Click the **Undo** .

❷ Click **Clear**.

Note: If the data deletion was the most recent action you performed, you can undo it by pressing Ctrl *+* Z *or by clicking* **Undo** *( ).*

● Excel restores the data to the cell.

When I delete cell data, Excel keeps the cell formatting intact. Is it possible to delete the data and the formatting?
Yes. Excel offers a command that deletes everything from a cell. First, select the cell with the data and formatting that you want to delete. Click **Home**, click , and then click **Clear All**. Excel removes both the data and the formatting from the selected cell.

Is it possible to delete just a cell's formatting?
Yes. Excel offers a command that deletes just the cell formatting while leaving the cell data intact. Select the cell with the formatting that you want to delete. Click **Home**, click , and then click **Clear Formats**. Excel removes just the formatting from the selected cell.

Chapter 3

Working with Excel Ranges

In Excel, a *range* is a collection of two or more cells that you work with as a group rather than separately. This enables you to fill the range with values, move or copy the range, sort the range data, filter the range to show only certain values, insert and delete ranges, hide entire rows or columns, and merge two or more cells. You learn these and other range techniques in this chapter, and in later chapters you learn techniques such as formatting a range, applying a formula to a range, and building a chart from a range.

Select a Range

To work with a range in Excel, you must select the cells that you want to include in the range. After you select the range, you can fill it with data, move or copy it to another part of the worksheet, format the cells, delete the data, and so on. You can select a range as a rectangular group of cells, as a collection of individual cells, or as an entire row or column. It is almost always easiest to select a range using the mouse, but Excel does offer a few keyboard shortcuts for selecting ranges, as described in the Tip on the next page.

Select a Range

Select a Rectangular Range

1. Position ✛ over the first cell you want to include in the range.

2. Click and drag ✛ over the cells that you want to include in the range.

● Excel selects the cells.

3. Release the mouse button to end the range selection.

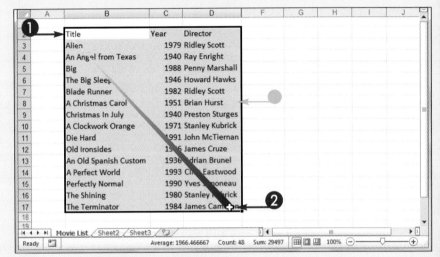

Select a Range of Individual Cells

1. Click in the first cell that you want to include in the range.

2. Hold down Ctrl and click in each of the other cells that you want to include in the range.

● Each time you click in a cell, Excel adds it to the range.

3. Release Ctrl to end the range selection.

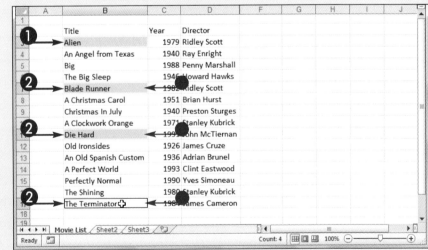

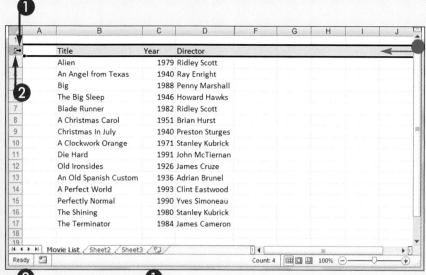

Select an Entire Row

① Position ✛ over the header of the row you want to select.

✛ changes to ➡.

② Click the row header.

● Excel selects the entire row.

To select multiple rows, click and drag across the row headers or hold down `Ctrl` and click each row header.

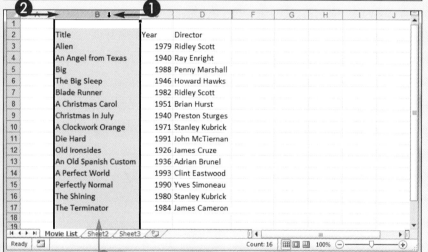

Select an Entire Column

① Position ✛ over the header of the column you want to select.

✛ changes to ⬇.

② Click the column header.

● Excel selects the entire column.

To select multiple columns, click and drag across the column headers, or hold down `Ctrl` and click each column header.

Simplify It

Are there keyboard techniques I can use to select a range?
Yes. To select a rectangular range, navigate to the first cell that you

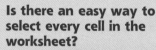

want to include in the range, hold down `Shift`, and then press ⬅ or ⬇ to extend the selection. To select an entire row, navigate to any cell in the row and press `Shift` + `Spacebar`. To select an entire column, navigate to any cell in the column and then press `Ctrl` + `Spacebar`.

Is there an easy way to select every cell in the worksheet?
Yes. Excel offers two methods you can use. Either press `Ctrl` + `A`, or click the **Select All** button (▣) in the upper left corner of the worksheet.

Fill a Range with the Same Data

If you need to fill a range with the same data, you can save time by getting Excel to fill the range for you. The most common method for filling a range in this way is to use Excel's AutoFill feature, which makes it easy to fill a vertical or horizontal range with the same value.

However, Excel also offers an alternative method that enables you to fill any selected range.

See "Select a Range," earlier in this chapter, to learn how to select a range of cells.

Fill a Range with the Same Data

Fill a Vertical or Horizontal Range

1 In the first cell of the range you want to work with, enter the data you want to fill.

2 Position ↔ over the bottom right corner of the cell.

↔ changes to +.

3 Click and drag + down to fill a vertical range or across to fill a horizontal range.

4 Release the mouse button.

● Excel fills the range with the initial cell value.

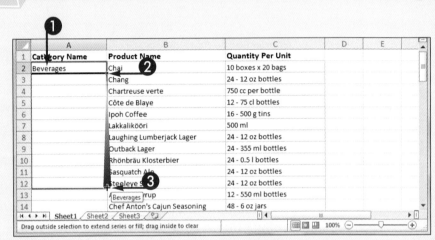

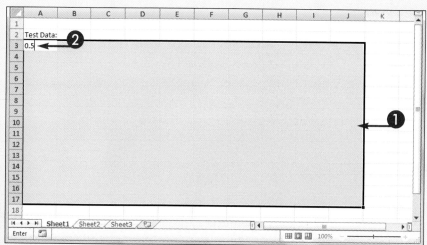

Fill a Selected Range

1 Select the range you want to fill.

2 Type the text, number, or other data.

3 Press Ctrl + Enter.

● Excel fills the range with the value you typed.

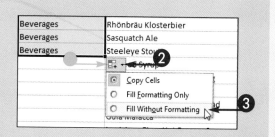

Simplify It

How do I fill a vertical or horizontal range without also copying the formatting of the original cell?
Follow these steps:

1 Perform Steps **1** to **4** to fill the data.

● Excel displays the AutoFill Options smart tag (⊞).

2 Click the AutoFill Options ▾.

3 Click **Fill Without Formatting**.

Excel removes the original cell's formatting from the copied cells.

Fill a Range with a Series of Values

If you need to fill a range with a series of values, you can save time by using Excel's AutoFill feature to create the series for you. AutoFill can fill a series of numeric values such as 5, 10, 15, 20, and so on; a series of date values such as January 1, 2011, January 2, 2011, and so on; or a series of alphanumeric values such as Chapter 1, Chapter 2, Chapter 3, and so on.

You can also create your own series with a custom step value, which determines the numeric difference between each item in the series.

Fill a Range with a Series of Values

AutoFill a Series of Numeric, Date, or Alphanumeric Values

1 Click in the first cell and type the first value in the series.

2 Click in an adjacent cell and type the second value in the series.

3 Select the two cells.

4 Position ⊕ over the bottom right corner of the second cell.

  ⊕ changes to +.

5 Click and drag + down to fill a vertical range or across to fill a horizontal range.

● As you drag through each cell, Excel displays the series value that it will add to the cell.

6 Release the mouse button.

● Excel fills the range with a series that continues the pattern of the initial two cell values.

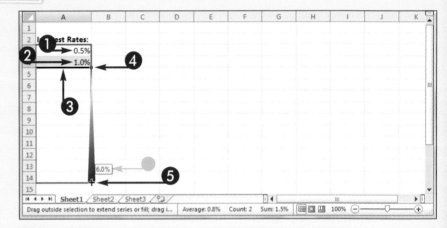

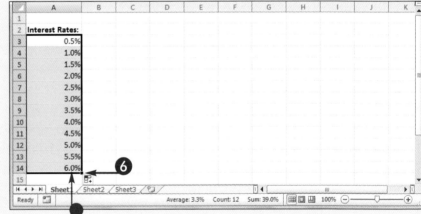

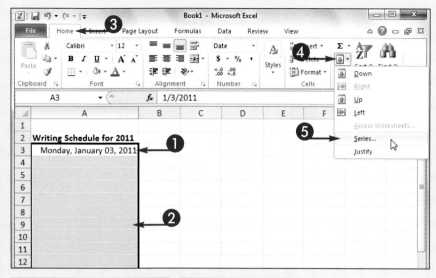

Fill a Custom Series of Values

❶ Click in the first cell and type the first value in the series.

❷ Select the range you want to fill, including the initial value.

❸ Click the **Home** tab.

❹ Click **Fill** (⊞).

❺ Click **Series**.

The Series dialog box appears.

❻ In the Type group, select the type of series you want to fill (◎ changes to ◉).

❼ If you selected **Date** in Step **6**, select an option in the **Date unit** group (◎ changes to ◉).

❽ In the Step value text box, type the value you want to use.

❾ Click **OK**.

● Excel fills the range with the series you created.

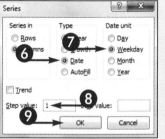

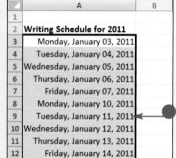

Simplify It

Can I create my own AutoFill series?
Yes. You can create a custom list. When you add the first value in your custom list, you can then use AutoFill to fill a range with the rest of the series. Follow these steps:

❶ Click the **File** tab.

❷ Click **Options**.

❸ Click **Advanced**.

❹ Click **Edit Custom Lists**.

❺ Click **NEW LIST**.

❻ In the List entries box, type each item in your list, and press Enter after each item.

❼ Click **Add**.

❽ Click **OK**.

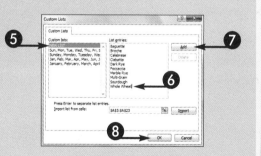

Move or Copy a Range

You can restructure or reorganize a worksheet by moving an existing range to a different part of the worksheet. For example, if you have two related ranges that are far apart on the worksheet, you can move one of them so that the ranges appear close to each other.

You can also make a copy of a range, which is a useful technique if you require either a duplicate of the range elsewhere, or if you require a range that is similar to an existing range.

Move a Range

1️⃣ Select the range you want to move.

2️⃣ Position ⬚ over any outside border of the range.

⬚ changes to ⬚.

3️⃣ Click and drag the range to the new location.

⬚ changes to ⬚.

🔘 Excel displays an outline of the range.

⚫ Excel displays the address of the new location.

4️⃣ Release the mouse button.

⚫ Excel moves the range to the new location.

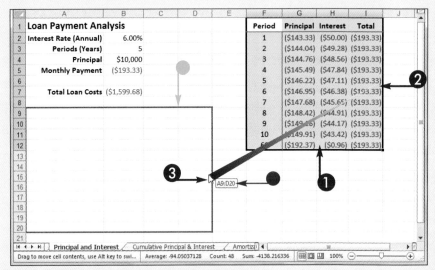

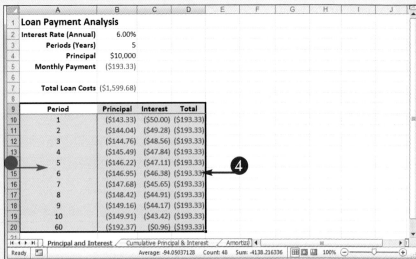

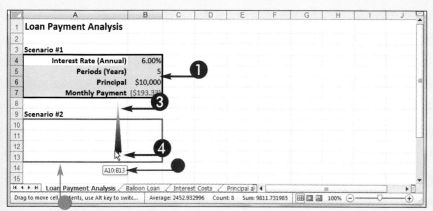

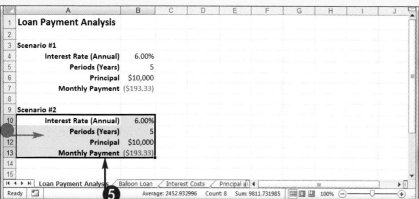

Copy a Range

❶ Select the range you want to copy.

❷ Press and hold **Ctrl**.

❸ Position ✛ over any outside border of the range.

✛ changes to ↖.

❹ Click and drag the range to the location where you want the copy to appear.

● Excel displays an outline of the range.

● Excel displays the address of the new location.

❺ Release the mouse button.

❻ Release **Ctrl**.

● Excel creates a copy of the range in the new location.

Can I move or copy a range to another worksheet?
Yes. Click and drag the range as described in this section. Remember to hold down **Ctrl** if you are copying the range. Press and hold **Alt** and then drag the mouse pointer over the tab of the sheet you want to use as the destination. Excel displays the worksheet. Release **Alt** and then drop the range on the worksheet.

Can I move or copy a range to another workbook?
Yes. If you can see the other workbook on-screen, click and drag the range as described in this section, and then drop it on the other workbook. Remember to hold down **Ctrl** if you are copying the range. Otherwise, select the range, click the **Home** tab, click **Cut** (✂) to move the range or **Copy** (📋) to copy it, switch to the other workbook, select the cell where you want the range to appear, click **Home**, and then click **Paste** (📋).

Insert a Row or Column

You can insert a row or column into your existing worksheet data to accommodate more information. This is particularly useful if the information you need to add fits naturally within the existing data, rather than at the end.

When you insert a row, Excel shifts the existing rows down, so you must first determine the row above where you want your new row to appear. Similarly, when you insert a column, Excel shifts the existing columns to the right, so you must first determine the column to the left of where you want your new column to appear.

Insert a Row or Column

Insert a Row

1. Click in any cell in the row above where you want to insert the new row.

2. Click the **Home** tab.

3. Click the **Insert** ⬜.

4. Click **Insert Sheet Rows**.

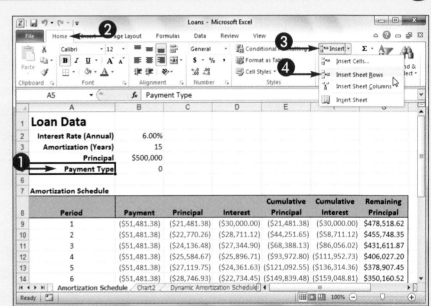

- Excel inserts the new row.
- The rows below the new row are shifted down.

5. Click the **Format** smart tag (⬧▾).

6. Select a formatting option for the new row (◎ changes to ◉).

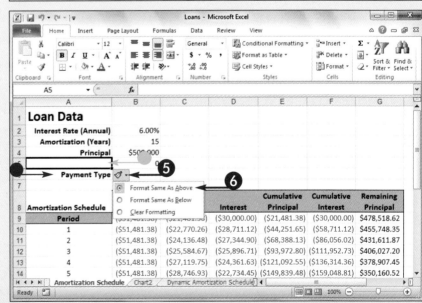

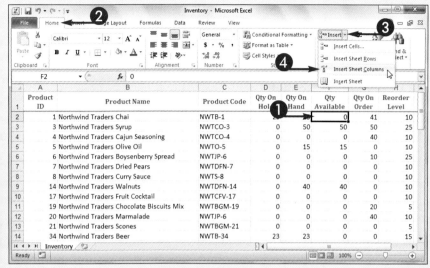

Insert a Column

1 Click any cell in the row to the left of where you want to insert the new column.

2 Click the **Home** tab.

3 Click the **Insert** ⊡.

4 Click **Insert Sheet Columns**.

● Excel inserts the new column.

● The columns to the right of the new column are shifted to the right.

5 Click the **Format** smart tag (⌧▾).

6 Select a formatting option for the new column (◎ changes to ◉).

Can I insert more than one row or column at a time?

Yes. You can insert as many new rows or columns as you need. First, select the same number of rows or columns that you want to insert. (See "Select a Range" earlier in this chapter to learn how to select rows and columns.) For example, if you want to insert four rows, select four existing rows. Follow Steps **2** to **4** in "Insert a Row" to insert rows, or Steps **2** to **4** in "Insert a Column" to insert columns.

Insert a Cell or Range

If you need to add data to an existing range, you can insert a single cell or a range of cells within that range. When you insert a cell or range, Excel shifts the existing data to accommodate the new cells.

Excel can either shift the existing data down or to the right. Therefore, you need to decide in advance where you want the new range to be inserted. You then tell Excel where you want the insertion to take place by selecting existing data either below or to the right of where you want the new range to appear.

Insert a Cell or Range

1 Select the cell or range where you want the inserted cell or range to appear.

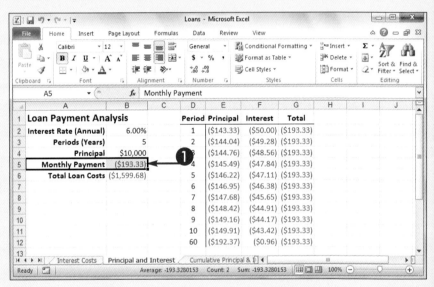

2 Click the **Home** tab.

3 Click the **Insert** ▾.

4 Click **Insert Cells**.

> **Note:** You can also press
> Ctrl + Shift + =.

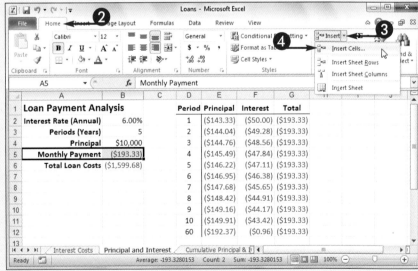

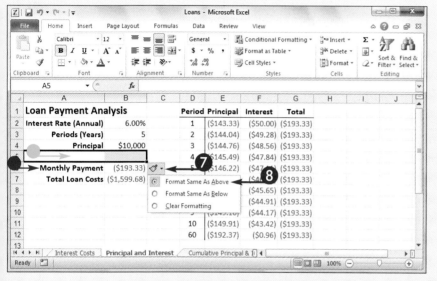

The Insert dialog box appears.

5 Select the option that corresponds to how you want Excel to shift the existing cells to accommodate your new cells (◎ changes to ◉).

Note: *In most cases, if you selected a horizontal range, click the **Shift cells down** option; if you selected a vertical range, click the **Shift cells right** option.*

6 Click **OK**.

Excel inserts the cell or range.

The existing data is shifted down (in this case) or to the right.

7 Click the **Format** smart tag (◇-).

8 Select a formatting option for the new row (◎ changes to ◉).

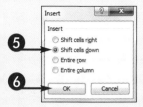

Under what circumstances would I insert a cell or range instead of inserting an entire row or column?
In most cases, it is better to insert a cell or range when you have other data either to the left or right of the existing range, or above or below the range. For example, if you have data to the left or right of the existing range, inserting an entire row would create a gap in the other data.

How do I know which cells to select to get my inserted cell or range in the correct position?
The easiest way to do this is to select the existing cell or range that is exactly where you want the new cell or range to appear. For example, if you want the new range to be A5:B5 as shown in this section's example, you first select the existing A5:B5 range. When you insert the new range, Excel shifts the existing cells down (in this case) to accommodate it.

Delete Data from a Range

If your worksheet has a range that contains data you no longer need, you can delete that data. This helps to reduce worksheet clutter and makes your worksheet easier to read.

Note that the technique in this section only applies to deleting the data that exists within each cell in a selected range; it does not apply to deleting the actual range. If you want to delete cells and not just the data, see "Delete a Range" later in this chapter.

Delete Data from a Range

Delete Range Data

① Select the range that contains the data you want to delete.

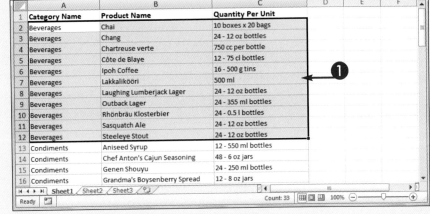

② Click the **Home** tab.

③ Click **Clear** (🖉).

④ Click **Clear Contents**.

● If you want to delete the range data and its formatting, click **Clear All** instead.

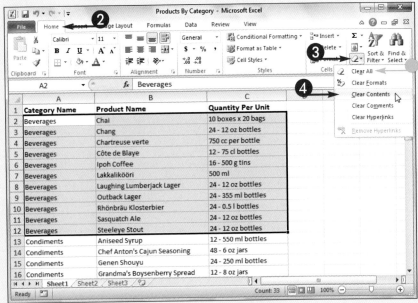

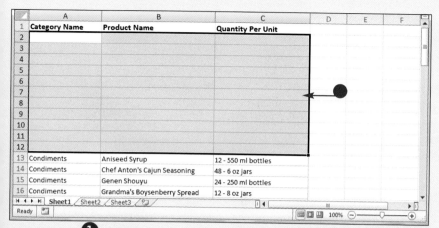

● Excel removes the range data.

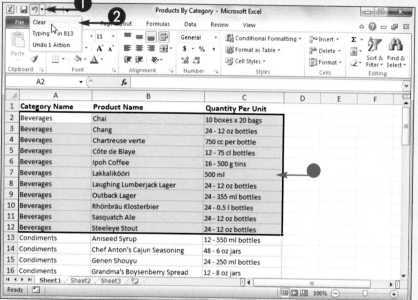

Undo Range Data Deletion

① Click the **Undo** ▾.

② Click **Clear**.

> *Note: If the data deletion was the most recent action you performed, you can undo it by pressing* Ctrl *+* Z *or by clicking* ***Undo*** *(⟲).*

● Excel restores the data to the range.

Are there faster ways to delete the data from a range?

Yes. Probably the fastest method is to select the range and then press Delete. You can also select the range, right-click any part of the range, and then click **Clear Contents**.

Is it possible to delete a cell's numeric formatting?

Yes. Select the range with the formatting that you want to delete, click **Home**, click ➡, and then click **Clear Formats**. Excel removes all the formatting from the selected range. If you prefer to delete only the numeric formatting, click **Home**, click the **Number Format** ▾, and then click **General**.

Delete
a Range

If your worksheet contains a range that you no longer need, you can delete that range. Note that when you delete a range, Excel deletes not just the data within the range, but the range cells themselves. Excel shifts the remaining worksheet data to replace the deleted range.

Note that the technique in this section deletes the actual cells from the selected range. If you want to delete only the data in the range, see "Delete Data from a Range" earlier in this chapter.

Delete a Range

① Select the range that you want to delete.

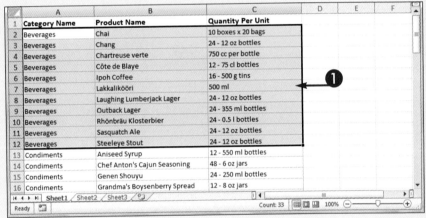

② Click the **Home** tab.

③ Click the **Delete** ⊡.

④ Click **Delete Cells**.

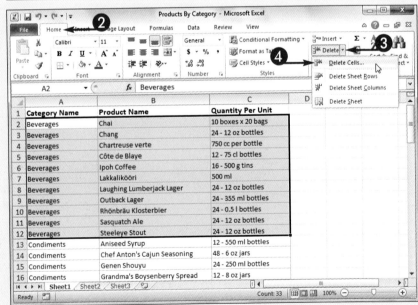

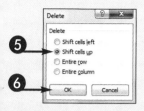

The Delete dialog box appears.

⑤ Select the option that corresponds to how you want Excel to shift the remaining cells after it deletes the range (◎ changes to ◉).

*Note: In most cases, if you have data below the selected range, click the **Shift cells up** option; if you have data to the right of the selected range, click the **Shift cells left** option.*

⑥ Click **OK**.

● Excel deletes the range and shifts the remaining data.

	A	B	C	D	E	F
1	Category Name	Product Name	Quantity Per Unit			
2	Condiments	Aniseed Syrup	12 - 550 ml bottles			
3	Condiments	Chef Anton's Cajun Seasoning	48 - 6 oz jars			
4	Condiments	Genen Shouyu	24 - 250 ml bottles			
5	Condiments	Grandma's Boysenberry Spread	12 - 8 oz jars			
6	Condiments	Gula Malacca	20 - 2 kg bags			
7	Condiments	Louisiana Fiery Hot Pepper Sauce	32 - 8 oz bottles			
8	Condiments	Louisiana Hot Spiced Okra	24 - 8 oz jars			
9	Condiments	Northwoods Cranberry Sauce	12 - 12 oz jars			
10	Condiments	Original Frankfurter grüne Soße	12 boxes			
11	Condiments	Sirop d'érable	24 - 500 ml bottles			
12	Condiments	Vegie-spread	15 - 625 g jars			
13	Confections	Chocolade	10 pkgs.			
14	Confections	Gumbär Gummibärchen	100 - 250 g bags			
15	Confections	Maxilaku	24 - 50 g pkgs.			
16	Confections	NuNuCa Nuß-Nougat-Creme	20 - 450 g glasses			

Are there faster ways to delete a range?
Yes. Probably the fastest method is to select the range and then press Ctrl + ⊟. You can also select the range, right-click any part of the range, and then click **Delete**. Both methods display the Delete dialog box.

How do I delete a row or column?
To delete a row, select any cell in the row, click the **Home** tab, click the **Delete** ⊡, and then click **Delete Sheet Rows**. To delete a column, select any cell in the column, click the **Home** tab, click the **Delete** ⊡, and then click or **Delete Sheet Columns**. Note, too, that you can delete multiple rows or columns by selecting at least one cell in each row or column.

Hide a Row or Column

If you do not need to see or work with a row or column temporarily, you can make your worksheet easier to read and to navigate by hiding the row or column.

Hiding a row or column is also useful if you are showing someone a worksheet that contains private or sensitive data that you do not want the person to see. For example, if a row or column contains salary data, passwords, or Social Security numbers, you should hide the row or column to protect this data from non-authorized viewers.

Hide a Row or Column

Hide a Row

① Click in any cell in the row you want to hide.

② Click the **Home** tab.

③ Click **Format**.

④ Click **Hide & Unhide**.

⑤ Click **Hide Rows**.

Note: You can also hide a row by pressing **Ctrl** + **9**.

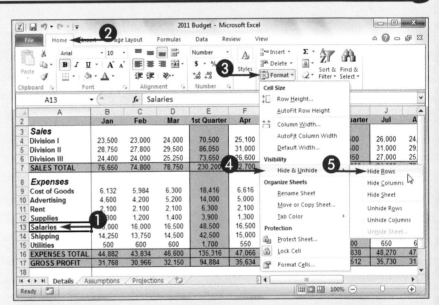

● Excel removes the row from the worksheet display.

● Excel displays a slightly thicker heading border between the surrounding rows to indicate that a hidden row lies between them.

Another way to hide a row is to move ⇧ over the bottom edge of the row heading (⇧ changes to +) and then click and drag the edge up until the height displays 0.

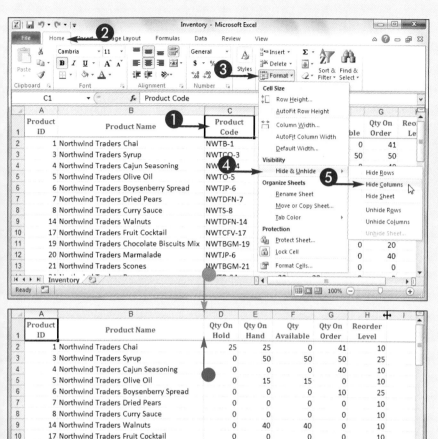

Hide a Column

1 Click in any cell in the column you want to hide.

2 Click the **Home** tab.

3 Click **Format**.

4 Click **Hide & Unhide**.

5 Click **Hide Columns**.

Note: You can also hide a column by pressing Ctrl + 0 *.*

● Excel removes the column from the worksheet display.

● Excel displays a slightly thicker heading border between the surrounding columns to indicate that a hidden column lies between them.

Another way to hide a column is to move ⊕ over the right edge of the column heading (⊕ changes to ┿) and then click and drag the edge left until the width displays 0.

How do I display a hidden row or column?

To display a hidden row, select the row above and the row below the hidden row, click **Home**, click **Format**, click **Hide & Unhide**, and then click **Unhide Rows**. Alternatively, move ⊕ between the headings of the selected rows (⊕ changes to ╪) and then double-click. To unhide row 1, right-click the top edge of the row 2 header and then click **Unhide**.

To display a hidden column, select the column to the left and the column to the right of the hidden column, click Home, click Format, click Hide & Unhide, and then click Unhide Columns. Alternatively, move ⊕ between the headings of the selected columns (⊕ changes to ┥┝) and then double-click. To unhide column A, right-click the left edge of the column B header and then click Unhide.

Freeze Rows or Columns

As you vertically scroll a worksheet, you can keep your column labels in view by freezing the row or rows that contain the labels. This makes it easier to review and edit the existing data and to insert new data to the worksheet because you can always see the column labels.

If your worksheet also includes row labels, you can keep those labels in view as you horizontally scroll the worksheet by freezing the column or columns that contain the labels.

Freeze Rows or Columns

Freeze Rows

① Scroll the worksheet so that the row or rows that you want to freeze are visible.

② Position ⊕ over the horizontal split bar (▭).

⊕ changes to ↕.

③ Click and drag ↕ and drop it below the row you want to freeze.

⬤ Excel splits the worksheet into two horizontal panes.

④ Click the **View** tab.

⑤ Click **Freeze Panes**.

⑥ Click **Freeze Panes**.

⬤ If you want to freeze just the first row, you can bypass Steps **1** to **3** and click the **Freeze Top Row** command.

Excel freezes the panes.

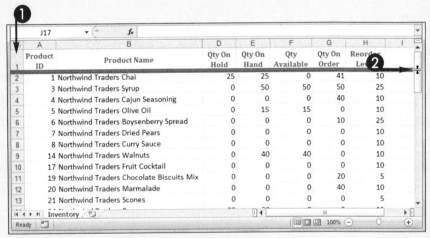

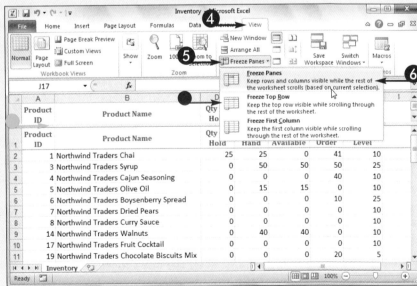

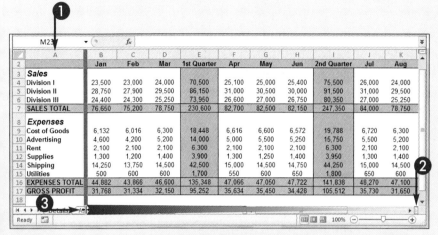

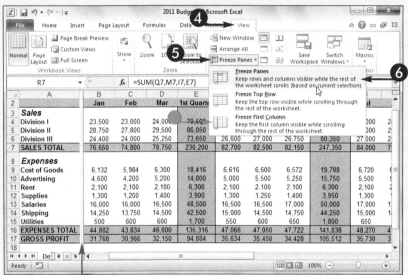

Freeze Columns

① Scroll the worksheet so that the column or columns that you want to freeze are visible.

② Position ⊕ over the vertical split bar (▯).

⊕ changes to ⊬.

③ Click and drag ⊬ and drop it on the right edge of the column you want to freeze.

● Excel splits the worksheet into two vertical panes.

④ Click the **View** tab.

⑤ Click **Freeze Panes**.

⑥ Click **Freeze Panes**.

● If you want to freeze just the first column, you can bypass Steps **1** to **3** and click the **Freeze First Column** command.

● Excel freezes the panes.

Simplify It

Can I adjust the position of a frozen row or column?
Yes. Begin by unfreezing the panes: Click **View**, click **Freeze Panes**, and then click **Unfreeze Panes**. Excel unfreezes the panes and displays the split bar. Click and drag the split bar to the new location. Click **View**, click **Freeze Panes**, and then click **Freeze Panes**.

How do I unfreeze a row or column?
If you no longer require a row or column to be frozen, you can unfreeze it by clicking **View**, clicking **Freeze Panes**, and then clicking **Unfreeze Panes**. If you no longer want your worksheet split into two panes, click **View** and then click **Split** (▤).

Merge Two or More Cells

You can create a single large cell by merging two or more cells. For example, it is common to merge some of the top row of cells to use as a worksheet title. Another common reason for merging cells is to create a label that applies to multiple columns of data. This can make your worksheet easier to read because it makes it clear that the label applies to multiple columns instead of just a single column.

Merge Two or More Cells

1 Select the cells that you want to merge.

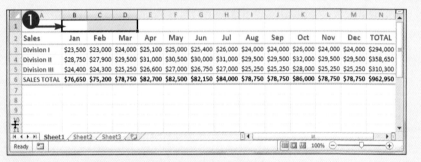

2 Click the **Home** tab.

3 Click the **Merge and Center** ⬚.

4 Click **Merge Cells**.

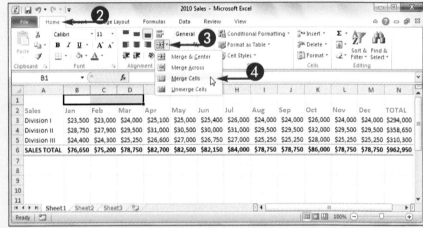

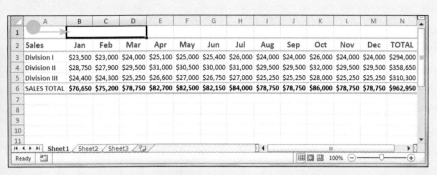

● Excel merges the selected cells into a single cell.

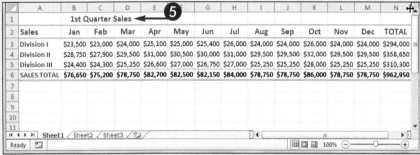

⑤ Type your text in the merged cell.

How do I center text across multiple columns?
This is a useful technique for your worksheet titles or headings. You can center a title across the entire worksheet, or you can center a heading across the columns that it refers to. Follow Steps **1** to **3** and then click **Merge & Center**. Excel creates the merged cell and formats the cell with the Center alignment option. Any text you enter into the merged cell appears centered within the cell.

Transpose Rows and Columns

You can use Excel's Transpose command to easily turn a row of data into a column of data, or a column of data into a row of data. You can also transpose rows and columns together in a single command, which is handy when you need to restructure a worksheet.

Transpose Rows and Columns

① Select the range that includes the data you want to transpose.

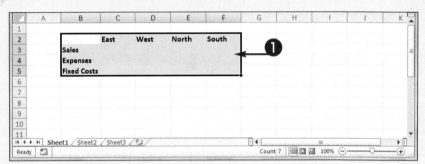

② Click the **Home** tab.

③ Click **Copy** (📋).

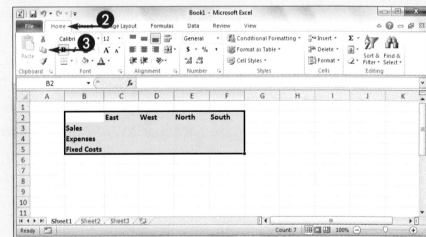

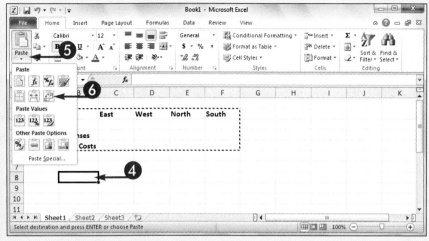

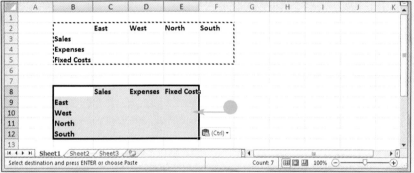

4 Click where you want the transposed range to appear.

5 Click the **Paste** ⊡.

6 Click **Transpose** (📋).

● Excel transposes the data and then pastes it to the worksheet.

How do I know which cells to select?
The range you select before copying depends on what you want to transpose. If you want to transpose a single horizontal or vertical range of cells, then select just that range. If you want to transpose a horizontal range of cells and a vertical range of cells at the same time, select the range that includes all the cells, as shown in this section's example.

Can I transpose range values as well as range labels?
Yes, Excel's Transpose command works with text, numbers, dates, formulas, and any other data that you can add to a cell. So if you have a rectangular region of data that includes row labels, column labels, and cell values within each row and column, you can select the entire range and transpose it.

Chapter 4

Working with Range Names

You can make it easier to navigate Excel worksheets and build Excel formulas by applying names to your ranges.

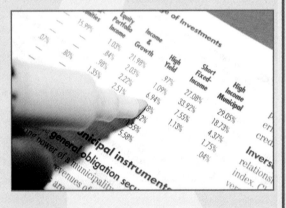

A *range name* is a text label that you apply to a single cell or to a range of cells. Once you have defined a name for a range, you can use that name in place of the range coordinates, which has several benefits. For example, range names are more intuitive than range coordinates, particularly in formulas; range names are more accurate than range coordinates; range names are easier to remember than range coordinates; and range names make it easier to navigate a worksheet.

This chapter explains range names and shows you how to define, edit, and use range names.

Define a Range Name

Before you can use a range name in your formulas or to navigate a worksheet, you must first define the range name. You can define as many names as you need, and you can even define multiple names for the same range.

You can create range names by hand, or you can get Excel to create the names for you automatically based on the existing text labels in a worksheet. For the latter, see "Use Worksheet Text to Define a Range Name."

Define a Range Name

① Select the range you want to name.

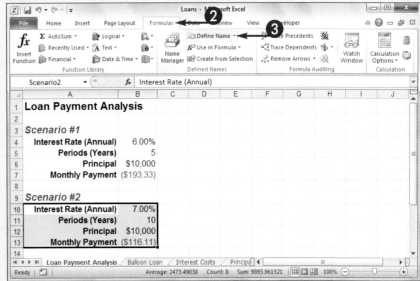

② Click the **Formulas** tab.

③ Click **Define Name**.

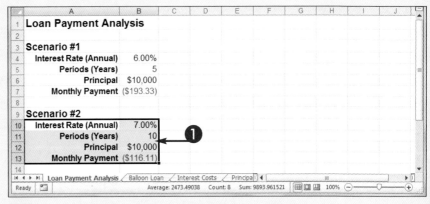

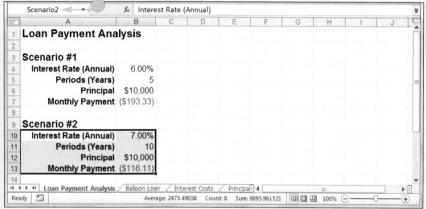

The New Name dialog box appears.

④ Type the name you want to use into the **Name** text box.

Note: *The first character of the name must be a letter or an underscore (_). The name cannot include spaces or cell references, and it cannot be any longer than 255 characters.*

⑤ Click **OK**.

Excel assigns the name to the range.

● The new name appears in the Name box whenever the range is selected.

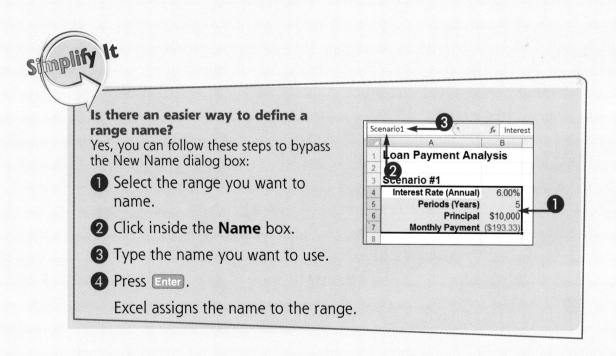

Is there an easier way to define a range name?

Yes, you can follow these steps to bypass the New Name dialog box:

❶ Select the range you want to name.

❷ Click inside the **Name** box.

❸ Type the name you want to use.

❹ Press Enter.

Excel assigns the name to the range.

Use Worksheet Text to Define a Range Name

If you have several ranges to name, you can speed up the process by getting Excel to create the names for you automatically based on the range's text labels.

Text labels make a worksheet easier to read and understand, but in this section you see that they also make it easier to define range names.

For example, if you have a column of sales data that has the label "Sales" on top, Excel can automatically apply the name "Sales" to that range. You can create range names from worksheet text when the labels are in the top or bottom row of the range, or the left or right column of the range.

Use Worksheet Text to Define a Range Name

1 Select the range or ranges you want to name.

● Be sure to include the text labels you want to use for the range names.

2 Click the **Formulas** tab.

3 Click **Create from Selection**.

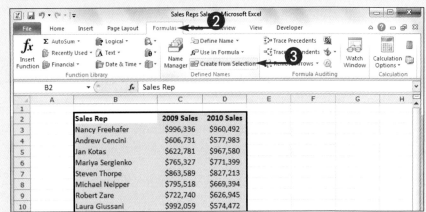

④

⑤

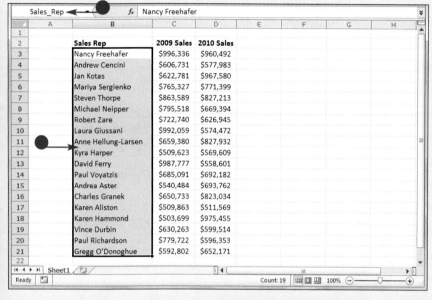

The Create Names from Selection dialog box appears.

④ Select the setting or settings that correspond to where the text labels are located in the selected range (☐ changes to ☑).

If Excel has activated a check box that does not apply to your data, click it (☑ changes to ☐).

⑤ Click **OK**.

Excel assigns the text labels as range names.

● When you select one of the ranges, the range name assigned by Excel appears in the Name box.

Note: *If the label text contains any illegal characters, such as a space, Excel replaces each of those characters with an underscore (_).*

Is there a faster way to run the Create from Selection command?
Yes, Excel offers a keyboard shortcut for the command. Select the range or ranges you want to work with and then press Ctrl + Shift + F3 . Excel displays the Create Names from Selection dialog box. Follow Steps **4** and **5** to create the range names.

Given a table with labels in the top row and left column, is there a way to automatically assign a name to the table data?
Yes. The table data refers to the range of cells that does not include the table headings in the top row and left column. To assign a name to the data range, type a label in the top left corner of the table. When you run the Create from Selection command on the entire table, Excel assigns the top left label to the data range, as shown here.

GDP_Growth		fx	2.9
A	B	C	D
1 GDP Growth	2004	2003	2002
2 Canada	2.9	2	3.4
3 France	2.3	0.8	1.2
4 Germany	1.6	0	0.2
5 United Kingdom	3.1	2.2	1.8
6 United States	4.2	3.1	1.9

Navigate a Workbook Using Range Names

One of the big advantages of defining range names is that they make it easier to navigate a worksheet. You can choose a range name from a list and Excel automatically selects the associated range. This is much faster than scrolling through a workbook by hand, or by entering a cell or range reference into Excel's Go To command.

Excel offers two methods for navigating a workbook using range names: the Name box and the Go To command.

Navigate a Workbook Using Range Names

Navigate Using the Name Box

1 Open the workbook that contains the range you want to work with.

2 Click the Name box ⊡.

3 Click the name of the range you want to select.

● Excel selects the range.

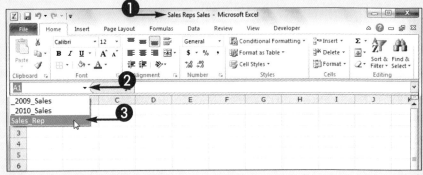

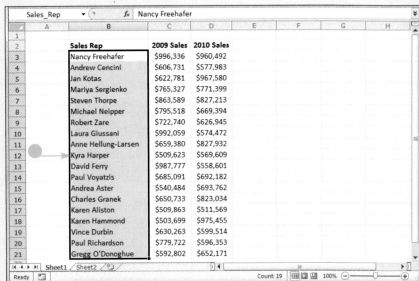

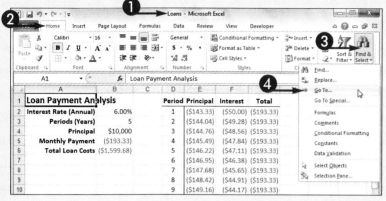

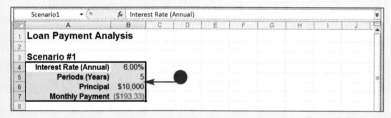

Navigate Using the Go To Command

1 Open the workbook that contains the range you want to work with.

2 Click the **Home** tab.

3 Click **Find & Select**.

4 Click **Go To**.

Note: You can also select the Go To command by pressing Ctrl + G.

The Go To dialog box appears.

5 Click the name of the range you want to select.

6 Click **OK**.

● Excel selects the range.

Is it possible to navigate to a named range in a different workbook?

Yes, but it is not easy or straightforward:

1 Follow Steps **1** to **4** on this page to display the Go To dialog box.

2 In the **Reference** text box, type the following:

'[workbook]worksheet'!name

Replace *workbook* with the file name of the workbook, *worksheet* with the name of the worksheet that contains the range, and *name* with the range name.

3 Click **OK**.

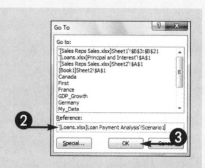

Change a Range Name

You can change any range name to a more suitable or accurate name. This is useful if you are no longer satisfied with the original name you applied to a range, if the data changes and the original name is no longer suitable for the new data, or if you do not like the name that Excel generated automatically from the worksheet labels.

If you want to change the range coordinates associated with a range name, see the second Tip on the next page.

Change a Range Name

① Open the workbook that contains the range name you want to change.

② Click the **Formulas** tab.

③ Click **Name Manager**.

The Name Manager dialog box appears.

④ Click the name you want to change.

⑤ Click **Edit**.

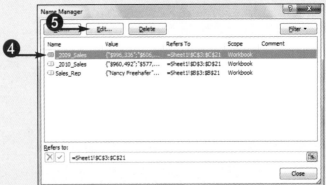

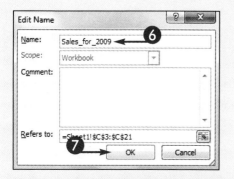

The Edit Name dialog box appears.

6 Use the **Name** text box to edit the name.

7 Click **OK**.

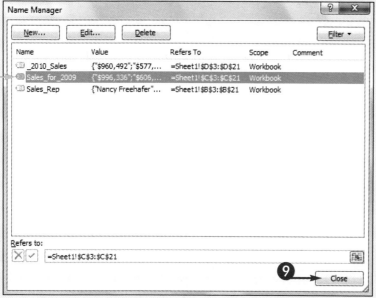

● The new name appears in the Name Manager dialog box.

8 Repeat Steps **4** to **7** to rename other ranges as needed.

9 Click **Close**.

Simplify It

Is there a faster method I can use to open the Name Manager dialog box?
Yes, Excel offers a shortcut key that enables you to bypass Steps **2** and **3**. Open the workbook that contains the range name you want to change, and then press Ctrl + F3. Excel opens the Name Manager dialog box.

Can I assign a name to a different range?
Yes. If you add another range to your workbook and you feel that an existing name would be more suited to that range, you can modify the name to refer to the new range. Follow Steps **1** to **5** to open the Edit Name dialog box. Click inside the **Refers to** reference box, and then click and drag the mouse ✛ on the worksheet to select the new range. Click **OK**.

Delete a Range Name

If you have a range name that you no longer need, you can use Excel's Name Manager to delete it. This is a good practice, because you do not want to have unused range names in a workbook. Getting rid of unneeded range names reduces clutter in the Name Manager dialog box, and it also makes the Name box easier to navigate. It is also a good idea to delete unused range names because you may need to reuse the names for different ranges later on.

Delete a Range Name

① Open the workbook that contains the range name you want to delete.

② Click the **Formulas** tab.

③ Click **Name Manager**.

Note: You can also select the Name Manager command by pressing **Ctrl** + **F3**.

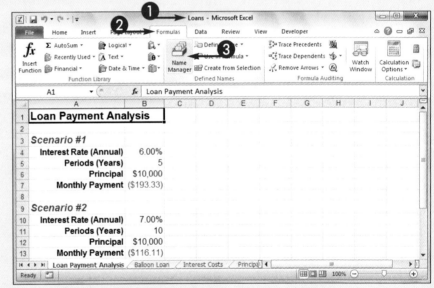

The Name Manager dialog box appears.

④ Click the name you want to delete.

⑤ Click **Delete**.

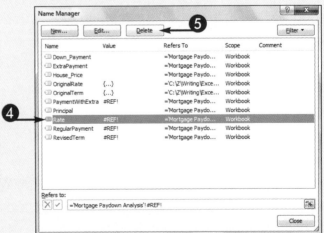

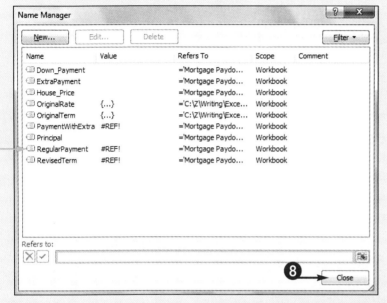

Excel asks you to confirm the deletion.

⑥ Click **OK**.

● Excel deletes the range name.

⑦ Repeat Steps **4** to **6** to delete other range names as needed.

⑧ Click **Close**.

Is there a faster way to delete multiple range names?
Yes, you can delete two or more range names at once. First, follow Steps **1** to **3** to display the Name Manager dialog box. Next, select the range names you want to delete: To select consecutive names, click the first name you want to delete, hold down Shift, and then click the last name you want to delete; to select non-consecutive names, hold down Ctrl and click each name you want to delete. When you have selected the name you want to remove, click **Delete** and then click **OK** when Excel asks you to confirm the deletion.

Chapter 5

Formatting Excel Ranges

Microsoft Excel 2010 offers many commands and options for formatting ranges, and you learn about most of them in this chapter. For text, you learn how to change the font, the font size, the text color, and the text alignment, as well as how to center text across columns and rotate text within a cell. You also learn how to change the background color, apply a number format, apply an AutoFormat and a style, change the column width and row height, add borders, and more.

Change the Font and Font Size

When you work in an Excel worksheet, you can add visual appeal to a cell or range by changing the font and font size.

In this section, the term *font* is synonymous with *typeface*, and both refer to the overall look of each character. By default, Excel offers

nearly 200 different fonts in a wide variety of styles. Also, the font size is measured in *points*, where there are roughly 72 points in an inch. In some cases, formatting a range with a larger font size can make the range text easier to read.

① Select the range you want to format.

② Click the **Home** tab.

③ To change the typeface, click ⊡ in the **Font** list and then click the typeface you want to apply.

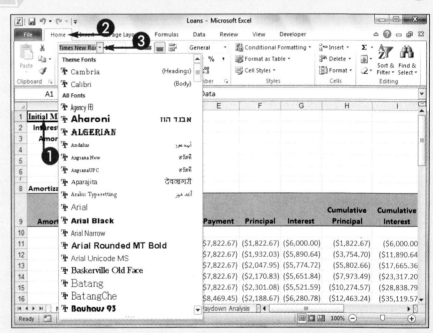

● Excel applies the font to the text in the selected range.

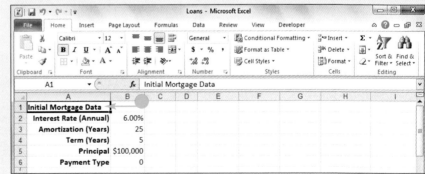

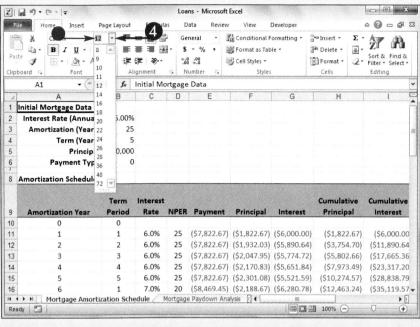

④ To change the font size, click
⊡ in the **Font Size** list and
then click the size you want to
apply.

● You can also type the size you
want in the Size text box.

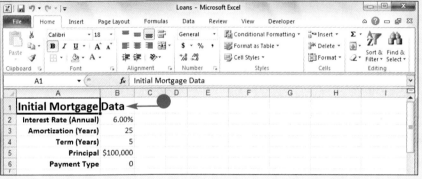

● Excel applies the font size to
the text in the selected range.

In the Theme Fonts section of the Font list, what do the designations Body and Headings mean?

When you create a workbook, Excel automatically applies a document theme to the workbook, and that theme includes predefined fonts. The theme's default font is referred to as Body, and it is the font used for regular worksheet text. Each theme also defines a Headings font, which Excel uses for cells formatted with a heading or title style.

Can I change the default font and font size?

Yes. Click the **File** tab and then click **Options** to open the Excel Options dialog box. Click the **General** tab, click the **Use this font** ⊡, and then click the typeface you want to use as the default. Click the **Font size** ⊡ and then click the size you prefer to use as the default. Click **OK**.

Apply Font Effects

You can improve the look and impact of text in an Excel worksheet by applying font effects to a range.

Excel's font effects include common formatting such as bold, italic, and underline, which are available on the Ribbon for easy application. Excel also offers a dialog box tab that includes many more font effects, including special effects such as strikethrough, superscripts, and subscripts.

In most cases, you should not need to apply more than one or two font effects at a time. If you use too many effects, it can make the text difficult to read.

Apply Font Effects

1. Select the range you want to format.

2. Click the **Home** tab.

3. To format the text as bold, click the **Bold** button (**B**).

● Excel applies the bold effect to the selected range.

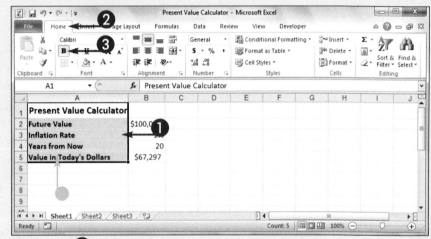

4. To format the text as italic, click the **Italic** button (*I*).

5. To format the text as underline, click the **Underline** button (U̲).

● Excel applies the effects to the selected range.

6. Click the **Font** dialog box launcher (▣).

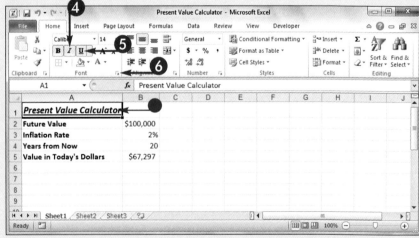

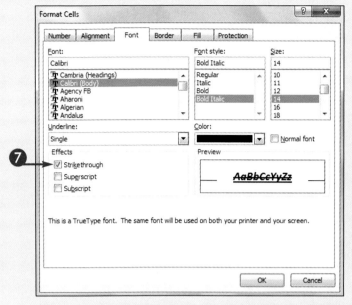

The Format Cells dialog box appears with the Font tab displayed.

⑦ To format the text as strikethrough, click **Strikethrough** (☐ changes to ☑).

⑧ To format the text as a superscript, click **Superscript** (☐ changes to ☑).

● To format the text as a subscript, click **Subscript** (☐ changes to ☑).

⑨ Click **OK**.

Excel applies the font effects.

Simplify It

Are there any font-related keyboard shortcuts I can use?
Yes. Excel supports the following font shortcuts:

Press	To
Ctrl + B	Toggle the selected range as bold
Ctrl + I	Toggle the selected range as italic
Ctrl + U	Toggle the selected range as underline
Ctrl + 5	Toggle the selected range as strikethrough

Change the Font Color

When you build an Excel worksheet, you can add visual interest to the sheet text by changing the font color.

By default, each Excel workbook comes with a theme applied, and you can change the font color by applying one of the colors from the workbook's theme. You learn more about workbook themes in Chapter 9.

You can also select a color from Excel's palette of standard colors, or from a custom color that you create yourself.

Change the Font Color

Select a Theme or Standard Color

1. Select the range you want to format.

2. Click the **Home** tab.

3. Click ⊡ in the **Font Color** list (🅰).

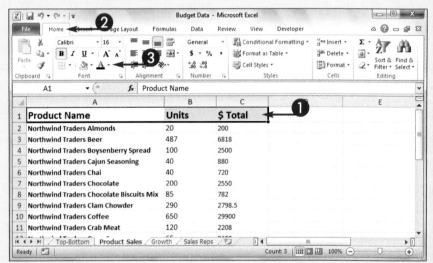

4. Click a theme color.

● Alternatively, click one of Excel's standard colors.

● Excel applies the color to the range text.

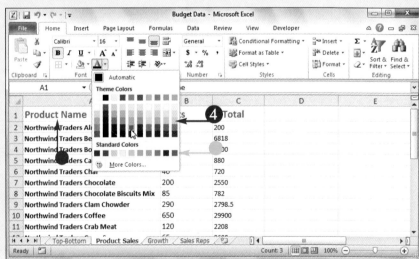

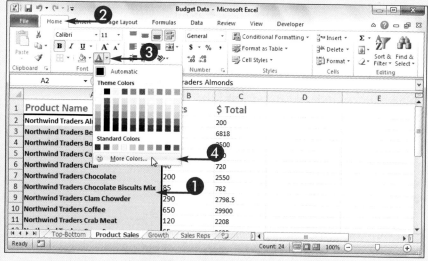

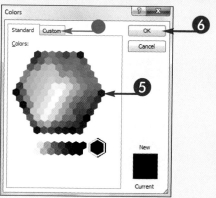

Select a Custom Color

① Select the range you want to format.

② Click the **Home** tab.

③ Click ⊡ in the **Font Color** list (⊿).

④ Click **More Colors**.

The Colors dialog box appears.

⑤ Click the color you want to use.

● You can also click the **Custom** tab and then either click the color you want or enter the values for the Red, Green, and Blue components of the color.

⑥ Click **OK**.

Excel applies the color to the selected range.

How can I make the best use of fonts in my documents?

● Do not use many different typefaces in a single document. Stick to one, or at most two, typefaces to avoid the ransom note look.

● Avoid overly decorative typefaces because they are often difficult to read.

● Use bold only for document titles, subtitles, and headings.

● Use italics only to emphasize words and phrases, or for the titles of books and magazines.

● Use larger type sizes only for document titles, subtitles, and, possibly, the headings.

● If you change the text color, be sure to leave enough contrast between the text and the background. In general, dark text on a light background is the easiest to read.

Align Text Within a Cell

You can make your worksheets easier to read by aligning text and numbers within each cell. By default, Excel aligns numbers with the right side of the cell, and it aligns text with the left side of the cell.

You can also align your data vertically within each cell. By default, Excel aligns all data with the bottom of each cell, but you can also align text with the top or middle.

Align Text Within a Cell

Align Text Horizontally

1 Select the range you want to format.

2 Click the **Home** tab.

3 In the Alignment group, click the horizontal alignment option you want to use:

Click **Align Text Left** (≣) to align data with the left side of each cell.

Click **Center** (≣) to align data with the center of each cell.

Click **Align Text Right** (≣) to align data with the right side of each cell.

Excel aligns the data horizontally within each selected cell.

● In this example, the data in the cells is centered.

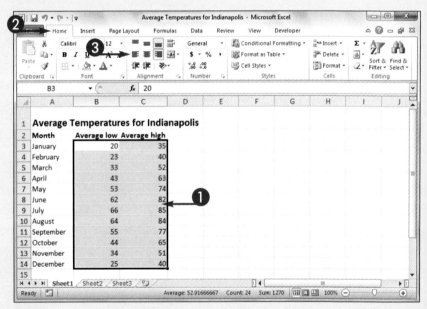

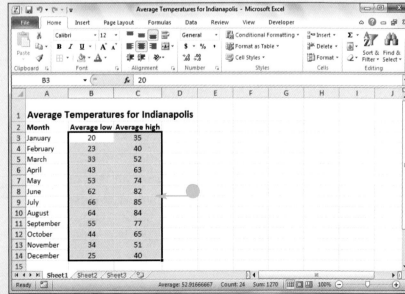

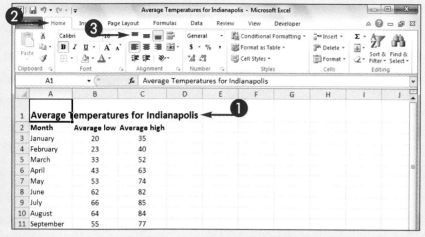

Align Text Vertically

1 Select the range you want to format.

2 Click the **Home** tab.

3 In the Alignment group, click the vertical alignment option you want to use:

Click **Top Align** (▤) to align data with the top of each cell.

Click **Middle Align** (▤) to align data with the middle of each cell.

Click **Bottom Align** (▤) to align data with the bottom of each cell.

Excel aligns the data vertically within each selected cell.

● In this example, the text is aligned with the middle of the cell.

Simplify It

How do I format text so that it aligns with both the left and right sides of the cell?

This is called *justified* text, and it is useful if you have a lot of text in one or more cells. Select the range, click the **Home** tab, and then click the dialog box launcher (▫) in the Alignment group. The Format Cells dialog box appears with the Alignment tab displayed. In the Horizontal list, click ▾ and then click **Justify**. Click **OK** to justify the cells.

How do I indent cell text?

Select the range you want to indent, click the **Home** tab, and then click the Alignment group's dialog box launcher (▫). In the Alignment tab, click the **Horizontal** list ▾ and then click **Left (Indent)**. Use the Indent text box to type the indent, in characters, and then click **OK**. You can also click the **Increase Indent** (▤) or **Decrease Indent** (▤) button in the Home tab's Alignment group.

Center Text Across Multiple Columns

You can make a worksheet more visually appealing and easier to read by centering text across multiple columns. This feature is most useful when you have text in a cell that you use as a label or title for a range. By centering the text across the range, it makes it easier to see that the label or title applies to the entire range.

1 Select a range that consists of the text you want to work with and the cells across which you want to center the text.

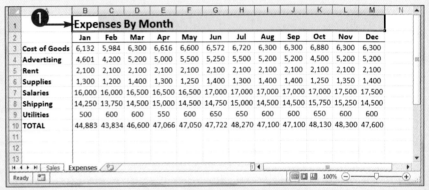

2 Click the **Home** tab.

3 In the Alignment group, click the dialog box launcher (⬚).

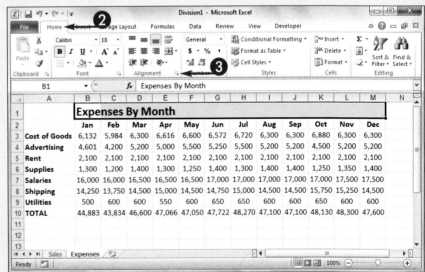

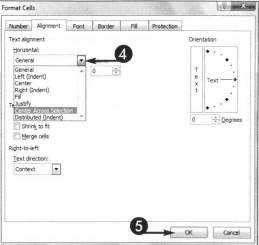

Excel opens the Format Cells dialog box with the Alignment tab displayed.

④ Click the **Horizontal** ⯆ and then click **Center Across Selection**.

⑤ Click **OK**.

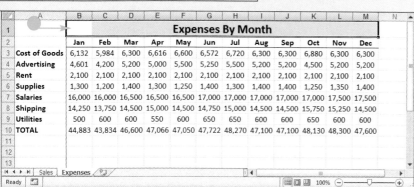

● Excel centers the text across the selected cells.

Simplify It

Is there an easier way to center text across multiple columns?
Yes, although it does require you to merge the selected cells into a single cell. (See Chapter 3 to learn more about merging cells.) Follow Steps **1** and **2** and then, in the Alignment group, click the **Merge & Center** button (⊞). Excel merges the selected cells into a single cell and centers the text within that cell.

Rotate Text Within a Cell

You can add visual interest to your text by slanting the text upward or downward in the cell. You can also use this technique to make a long column heading take up less horizontal space on the worksheet.

Excel offers several predefined rotations, such as Angle Counterclockwise, which angles text upward at a 45-degree angle; or Rotate Text Up, which displays the text vertically with the letters running from the bottom of the cell to the top. You can also make cell text angle upward or downward by specifying the degrees of rotation.

① Select the range containing the text you want to angle.

② Click the **Home** tab.

③ Click **Orientation** (⧉).

● If you want to use a predefined orientation, click one of the menu items and skip the rest of the steps.

④ Click **Format Cell Alignment**.

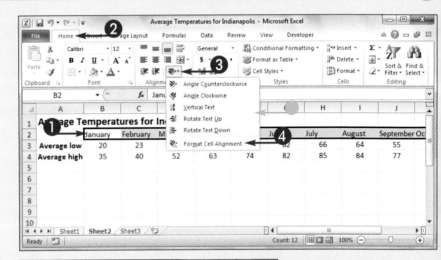

The Format Cells dialog box appears with the Alignment tab displayed.

⑤ Click an orientation marker.

● You can also use the Degrees spin box to type or click a degree of rotation. (See the Tip on the following page.)

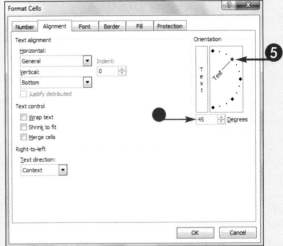

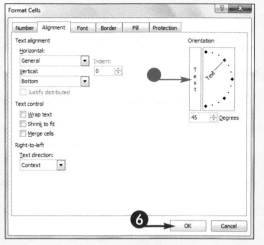

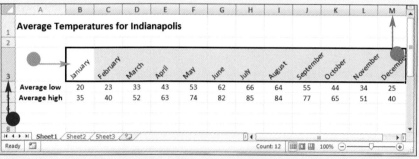

● You can click the vertical text area to display your text vertically instead of horizontally in the cell.

6 Click **OK**.

● Excel rotates the cell text.

● The row height automatically increases to contain the slanted text.

● You can reduce the column width to free up space and make your cells more presentable.

How does the Degrees spin box work?
If you use the Degrees spin box to set the text orientation, you can set the text orientation to a positive number, such as 25, and Excel angles the text in an upward direction. If you set the text orientation to a negative number, such as −40, Excel angles the text in a downward direction.

You can specify values in the range from 90 degrees (which is the same as clicking the Rotate Text Up command in the Orientation menu) to −90 degrees (which is the same as clicking the Rotate Text Down command).

Add a Background Color to a Range

You can make a range stand out from the rest of the worksheet by applying a background color to the range. For example, many people apply a background color to the labels in a range, which makes it easier to differentiate the labels from the data.

Perhaps the easiest way to change the background color is by applying a color from the set of 60 predefined colors that come with the workbook's theme. You can also choose a color from Excel's palette of standard colors, or from a custom color that you create yourself.

Add a Background Color to a Range

Select a Theme or Standard Color

1. Select the range you want to format.

2. Click the **Home** tab.

3. Click ⊡ in the **Fill Color** list (🖎).

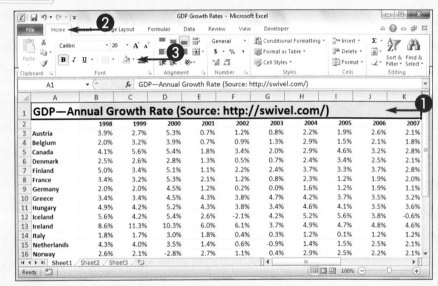

4. Click a theme color.

● Alternatively, click one of Excel's standard colors.

● Excel applies the color to the range text.

● To remove the background color from the range, click **No Fill**.

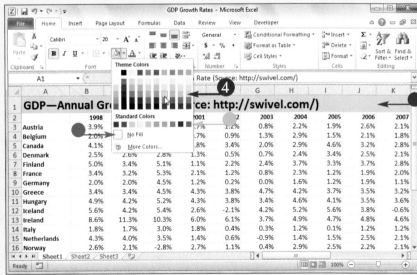

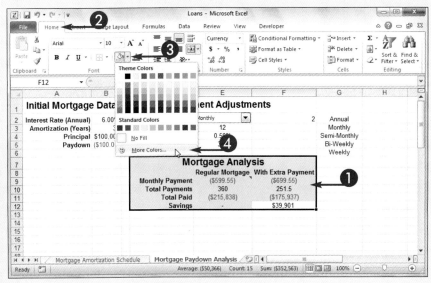

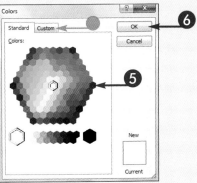

Select a Custom Color

1 Select the range you want to format.

2 Click the **Home** tab.

3 Click ⊡ in the **Fill Color** list (⬚).

4 Click **More Colors**.

The Colors dialog box appears.

5 Click the color you want to use.

● You can also click the **Custom** tab and then either click the color you want or enter the values for the Red, Green, and Blue components of the color.

6 Click **OK**.

Excel applies the color to the selected range.

Simplify It

Are there any pitfalls to watch out for when I apply background colors?
Yes. The biggest pitfall is applying a background color that clashes with the range text. For example, the default text color is black, so if you apply any dark background color, the text will be very difficult to read. Always use either a light background color with dark-colored text, or a dark background color with light-colored text.

Can I apply a background that fades from one color to another?
Yes. This is called a *gradient effect*. Select the range, click the **Home** tab, and then click the Font group's dialog box launcher (⬚). Click the **Fill** tab and then click **Fill Effects**. In the Fill Effects dialog box, use the **Color 1** ⊡ and the **Color 2** ⊡ to choose your colors. Click an option in the Shading styles section (○ changes to ◉), and then click **OK**.

Apply a Number Format

You can make your worksheet easier to read by applying a number format to your data. For example, if your worksheet includes monetary data, you can apply the Currency format to display each value with a dollar sign and two decimal places.

Excel offers ten number formats, most of which apply to numeric data. However, you can also apply the Date format to date data, the Time format to time data, and the Text format to text data.

Apply a Number Format

1 Select the range you want to format.

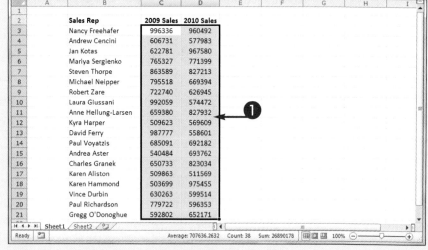

2 Click the **Home** tab.

3 Click the **Number Format** ⊡.

4 Click the number format you want to use.

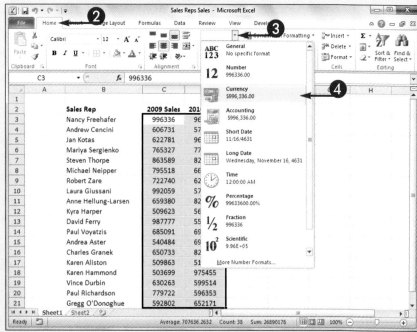

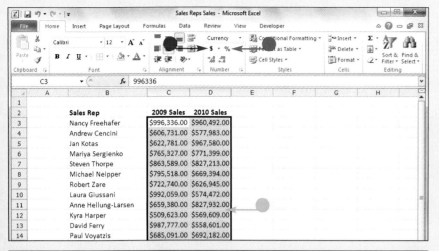

● Excel applies the number format to the selected range.

● For monetary values, you can also click **Accounting Number Format** ($).

● For percentages, you can also click **Percent Style** (%).

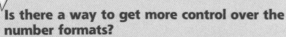

● For large numbers, you can also click **Comma Style** (,).

Simplify It

Is there a way to get more control over the number formats?

Yes. You can use the Format Cells dialog box to control properties such as the display of negative numbers, the currency symbol used, and how dates and times appear. Follow these steps:

① Select the range you want to format.

② Click the **Home** tab.

③ Click the Number group's dialog box launcher (□).

The Format Cells dialog box appears with the Number tab displayed.

④ In the Category list, click the type of number format you want to apply.

⑤ Use the controls that Excel displays to customize the number format.

The controls you see vary depending on the number format you chose in Step **4**.

⑥ Click **OK**.

Excel applies the number format.

Change the Number of Decimal Places Displayed

You can make your numeric values easier to read and interpret by adjusting the number of decimal places that Excel displays. For example, you might want to ensure that all dollar-and-cent values show two decimal places, while dollar-only values show no decimal places. Similarly, Excel often displays values with a large number of decimal places. If you do not require the extra decimals — for example, if the values are simple temperatures or interest rates — you can make them easier to read by reducing the number of decimals.

You can either decrease or increase the number of decimal places that Excel displays.

Change the Number of Decimal Places Displayed

Decrease the Number of Decimal Places

① Select the range you want to format.

② Click the **Home** tab.

③ Click the **Decrease Decimal** button (⌐.00).

● Excel decreases the number of decimal places by one.

④ Repeat Step **3** until you get the number of decimal places you want.

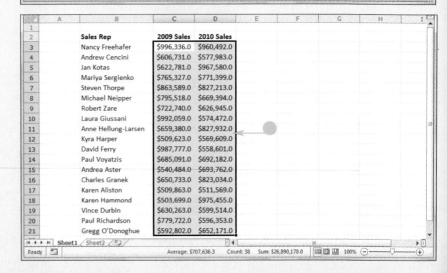

94

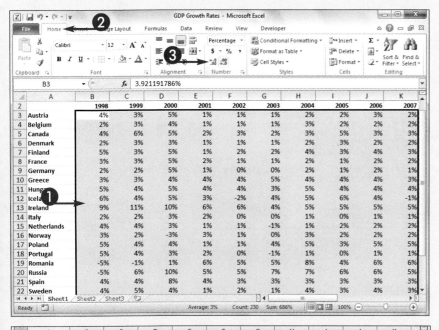

Increase the Number of Decimal Places

1. Select the range you want to format.

2. Click the **Home** tab.

3. Click the **Increase Decimal** button (⬚).

● Excel increases the number of decimal places by one.

4. Repeat Step **3** until you get the number of decimal places you want.

My range currently has values that display different numbers of decimal places. What happens when I change the number of decimal places?
In this situation, Excel uses the value that has the most displayed decimal places as the basis for formatting all the values. For example, if the selected range has values that display no, one, two, or four decimal places, Excel uses the value with four decimals as the basis. If you click **Decrease Decimal**, Excel displays every value with three decimal places; if you click **Increase Decimal**, Excel displays every value with five decimal places.

Apply an AutoFormat to a Range

You can save time when formatting your Excel worksheets by using the AutoFormat feature. This feature offers a number of predefined formatting options that you can apply to a range all at once. The formatting options include the number format, font, cell alignment, borders, patterns, row height, and column width.

The AutoFormats are designed for data in a tabular format, particularly where you have headings in the top row and left column, numeric data in the rest of the cells, and a bottom row that shows the totals for each column.

Apply an AutoFormat to a Range

1 Select the range you want to format.

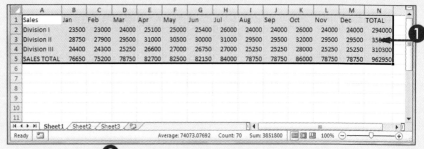

2 Click **AutoFormat** (⬚).

Note: See Chapter 1 to learn how to add a button to the Quick Access Toolbar. In this case, you must add the QuickFormat button.

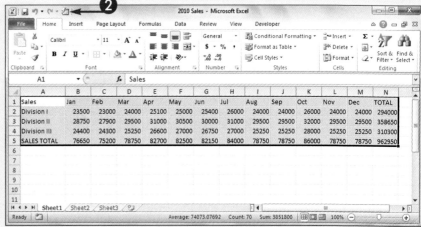

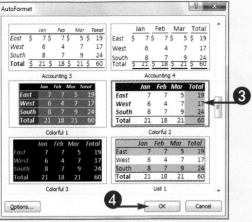

The AutoFormat dialog box appears.

3 In the Table format list, click the AutoFormat you want to use.

4 Click **OK**.

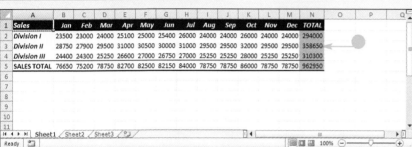

Excel applies the AutoFormat to the selected range.

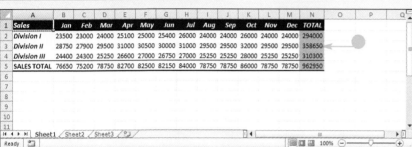
Simplify It

Is there a way to apply an AutoFormat without using some of its formatting?
Yes. Excel enables you to control all six formats that are part of each AutoFormat: Number, Font, Alignment, Border, Patterns, and Width/Height. Follow Steps **1** to **3** to choose the AutoFormat you want to apply. Click **Options** to expand the dialog box and display the Formats to apply group. Deselect the option for each format you do not want to apply (☑ changes to ☐), and then click **OK**.

How do I remove an AutoFormat?
If you do not like or no longer need the AutoFormat you applied to the cells, you can revert to a plain, unformatted state. Select the range and then click ☒ to display the AutoFormat dialog box. In the format list, click **None**, and then click **OK**. Excel removes the AutoFormat from the selected range.

Apply a Conditional Format to a Range

You can make a worksheet easier to analyze by applying a conditional format to a range. A *conditional format* is formatting that Excel applies only to cells that meet the condition you specify. For example, you can tell Excel to apply the formatting only if a cell's value is greater than some specified amount.

When you set up your conditional format, you can specify the font, border, and background pattern, which helps to ensure that the cells that meet your criteria stand out from the other cells in the range.

Apply a Conditional Format to a Range

❶ Select the range you want to work with.

❷ Click the **Home** tab.

❸ Click **Conditional Formatting**.

❹ Click **Highlight Cells Rules**.

❺ Click the operator you want to use for your condition.

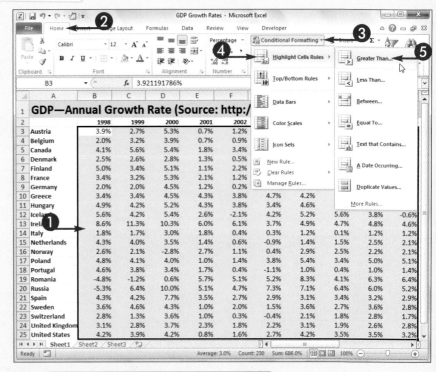

An operator dialog box appears, such as the Greater Than dialog box shown here.

❻ Type the value you want to use for your condition.

⬤ You can also click the collapse dialog box button (▣) and then click in a worksheet cell.

Depending on the operator, you may need to specify two values.

❼ Click this ▾ and then click the formatting you want to use.

⬤ To create your own format, click **Custom Format**.

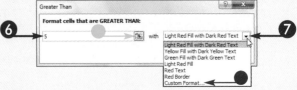

Greater Than

Format cells that are GREATER THAN:

| 5.0% | with | Light Red Fill with Dark Red Text |

⑧ ➤ OK   Cancel

⑧ Click **OK**.

● Excel applies the formatting to cells that meet your condition.

GDP—Annual Growth Rate (Source: http://swivel.com/)

	1998	1999	2000	2001	2002	2003	2004	2005	2006	2007
Austria	3.9%	2.7%	5.3%	0.7%	1.2%	0.8%	2.2%	1.9%	2.6%	2.1%
Belgium	2.0%	3.2%	3.9%	0.7%	0.9%	1.3%	2.9%	1.5%	2.1%	1.8%
Canada	4.1%	5.6%	5.4%	1.8%	3.4%	2.0%	2.9%	4.6%	3.2%	2.8%
Denmark	2.5%	2.6%	2.8%	1.3%	0.5%	0.7%	2.4%	3.4%	2.5%	2.1%
Finland	5.0%	3.4%	5.1%	1.1%	2.2%	2.4%	3.7%	3.3%	3.7%	2.8%
France	3.4%	3.2%	5.3%	2.1%	1.2%	0.8%	2.3%	1.2%	1.9%	2.0%
Germany	2.0%	2.0%	4.5%	1.2%	0.2%	0.0%	1.6%	1.2%	1.9%	1.1%
Greece	3.4%	3.4%	4.5%	4.3%	3.8%	4.7%	4.2%	3.7%	3.5%	3.2%
Hungary	4.9%	4.2%	5.2%	4.3%	3.8%	3.4%	4.6%	4.1%	3.5%	3.6%
Iceland	5.6%	4.2%	5.4%	2.6%	-2.1%	4.2%	5.2%	5.6%	3.8%	-0.6%
Ireland	8.6%	11.3%	10.3%	6.0%	6.1%	3.7%	4.9%	4.7%	4.8%	4.6%
Italy	1.8%	1.7%	3.0%	1.8%	0.4%	0.3%	1.2%	0.1%	1.2%	1.2%
Netherlands	4.3%	4.0%	3.5%	1.4%	0.6%	-0.9%	1.4%	1.5%	2.5%	2.1%
Norway	2.6%	2.1%	-2.8%	2.7%	1.1%	0.4%	2.9%	2.5%	2.2%	2.1%
Poland	4.8%	4.1%	4.0%	1.0%	1.4%	3.8%	5.4%	3.4%	5.0%	5.1%
Portugal	4.6%	3.8%	3.4%	1.7%	0.4%	-1.1%	1.0%	0.4%	1.0%	1.4%
Romania	-4.8%	-1.2%	0.6%	5.7%	5.1%	5.2%	8.3%	4.1%	6.3%	6.4%
Russia	-5.3%	6.4%	10.0%	5.1%	4.7%	7.3%	7.1%	6.4%	6.0%	5.2%
Spain	4.3%	4.2%	7.7%	3.5%	2.7%	2.9%	3.1%	3.4%	3.2%	2.9%
Sweden	3.6%	4.6%	4.3%	1.0%	2.0%	1.5%	3.6%	2.7%	3.6%	2.8%
Switzerland	2.8%	1.3%	3.6%	1.0%	0.3%	-0.4%	2.1%	1.8%	2.8%	1.7%
United Kingdom	3.1%	2.8%	3.7%	2.3%	1.8%	2.2%	3.1%	1.9%	2.6%	2.8%
United States	4.2%	3.9%	4.2%	0.8%	1.6%	2.7%	4.2%	3.5%	3.5%	3.2%

Sheet1 / Sheet2 / Sheet3

Ready   100%

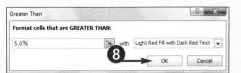

Simplify It

Can I set up more than one condition for a single range?
Yes. Excel enables you to specify multiple conditional formats. For example, you could set up one condition for cells that are greater than some value, and a separate condition for cells that are less than some other value. You can apply unique formats to each condition. Follow Steps **1** to **8** to configure the new condition.

How do I remove a conditional format from a range?
If you no longer require a conditional format, you can delete it. Follow Steps **1** to **3** to select the range and display the Conditional Formatting menu, and then click **Manage Rules**. Excel displays the Conditional Formatting Rules Manager dialog box. Click the conditional format you want to remove and then click **Delete Rule**.

Apply a Style to a Range

You can reduce the time it takes to format your worksheets by applying Excel's predefined styles to your ranges. Excel comes with more than 20 predefined styles for different worksheet elements such as headings, as well as two dozen styles associated with the current document theme.

Each style includes the number format, cell alignment, font typeface and size, border, and fill color.

Apply a Style to a Range

1 Select the range you want to format.

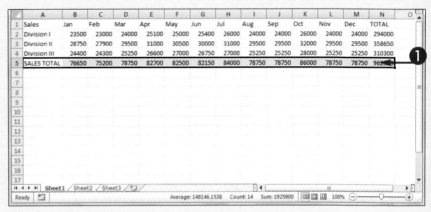

2 Click the **Home** tab.

3 Click **Cell Styles**.

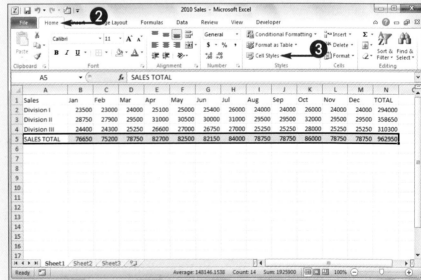

Excel displays the Cell Styles gallery.

④ Click the style you want to apply.

Note: *If the style is not exactly the way you want, you can right-click the style, click* **Modify**, *and then click* **Format** *to customize the style.*

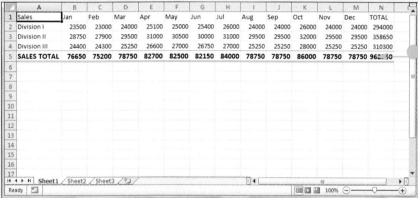

Excel applies the style to the range.

Are there styles I can use to format tabular data?
Yes. Excel comes with a gallery of table styles that offer formatting options that highlight the first row, apply different formats to alternating rows, and so on. Select the range that includes your data, click the **Home** tab, and then click **Format as Table**. In the gallery that appears, click the table format you want to apply.

Can I create my own style?
Yes. This is useful if you find yourself applying the same set of formatting options over and over. By saving those options as a custom style, you can apply it by following Steps **1** to **4**. Apply your formatting to a cell or range, and then select that cell or range. Click **Home**, click **Cell Styles**, and then click **New Cell Style**. In the Style dialog box, type a name for your style, and then click **OK**.

Change the Column Width

You can make a column of data easier to read by adjusting the column width. For example, if you have a large number or a long line of text in a cell, Excel may display only part of the cell value. To avoid this, you can increase the width of the column.

Similarly, if a column only contains a few characters in each cell, you can decrease the width to fit more columns on the screen.

Change the Column Width

1 Click in any cell in the column you want to resize.

2 Click the **Home** tab.

3 Click **Format**.

4 Click **Column Width**.

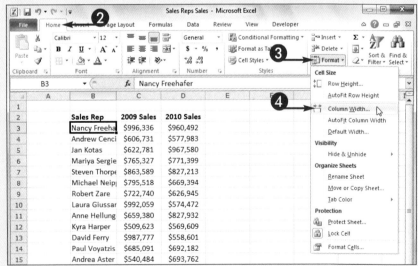

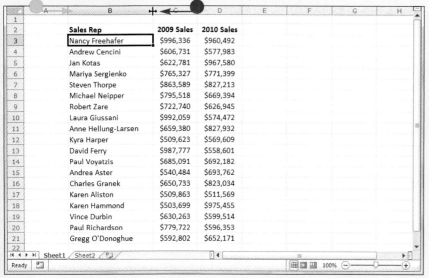

The Column Width dialog box appears.

⑤ In the Column width text box, type the width you want to use.

⑥ Click **OK**.

● Excel adjusts the column width.

● You can also move ⬚ over the right edge of the column heading (⬚ changes to ✛) and then click and drag the edge to set the width.

Simplify It

Is there an easier way to adjust the column width to fit the contents of a column?
Yes. You can use Excel's AutoFit feature, which automatically adjusts the column width to fit the widest item in a column. Click any cell in the column, click **Home**, click **Format**, and then click **AutoFit Column Width**. Alternatively, move ⬚ over the right edge of the column heading (⬚ changes to ✛) and then double-click.

Is there a way to change all the column widths at once?
Yes. Click ▭ (or press Ctrl + A) to select the entire worksheet, and then follow the steps in this section to set the width you prefer. If you have already adjusted some column widths and you want to change all the other widths, click **Home**, click **Format**, and then click **Default Width** to open the Standard Width dialog box. Type the new standard column width, and then click **OK**.

Standard Width	?	X
Standard column width:	10.38	
OK	Cancel	

Change the Row Height

You can make your worksheet more visually appealing by increasing the row heights to create more space. This is particularly useful in worksheets that are crowded with text. By increasing the row heights, you add white space above each cell, which makes the text easier to read.

If you want to change the row height to display multiline text within a cell, you must also turn on text wrapping within the cell. See "Wrap Text Within a Cell" later in this chapter.

Change the Row Height

1 Select a range that includes at least one cell in every row you want to resize.

2 Click the **Home** tab.

3 Click **Format**.

4 Click **Row Height**.

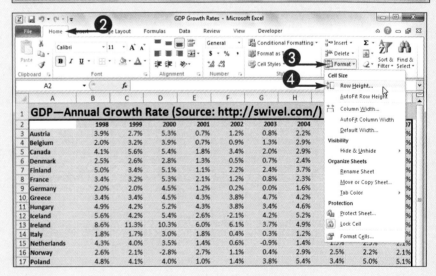

| Row Height | | | | ⑤ |
| Row height: | 18 | |

⑥ → OK   Cancel

	A	B	C	D	E	F	G	H	I	J	K
1	GDP—Annual Growth Rate (Source: http://swivel.com/)										
2		1998	1999	2000	2001	2002	2003	2004	2005	2006	2007
3	Austria	3.9%	2.7%	5.3%	0.7%	1.2%	0.8%	2.2%	1.9%	2.6%	2.1%
4	Belgium	2.0%	3.2%	3.9%	0.7%	0.9%	1.3%	2.9%	1.5%	2.1%	1.8%
5	Canada	4.1%	5.6%	5.4%	1.8%	3.4%	2.0%	2.9%	4.6%	3.2%	2.8%
6	Denmark	2.5%	2.6%	2.8%	1.3%	0.5%	0.7%	2.4%	3.4%	2.5%	2.1%
7	Finland	5.0%	3.4%	5.1%	1.1%	2.2%	2.4%	3.7%	3.3%	3.7%	2.8%
8	France	3.4%	3.2%	5.3%	2.1%	1.2%	0.8%	2.3%	1.2%	1.9%	2.0%
9	Germany	2.0%	2.0%	4.5%	1.2%	0.2%	0.0%	1.6%	1.2%	1.9%	1.1%
10	Greece	3.4%	3.4%	4.5%	4.3%	3.8%	4.7%	4.2%	3.7%	3.5%	3.2%
11	Hungary	4.9%	4.2%	5.2%	4.3%	3.8%	3.4%	4.6%	4.1%	3.5%	3.6%
12	Iceland	5.6%	4.2%	5.4%	2.6%	-2.1%	4.2%	5.2%	5.6%	3.8%	-0.6%
13	Ireland	8.6%	11.3%	10.3%	6.0%	6.1%	3.7%	4.9%	4.7%	4.8%	4.6%
14	Italy	1.8%	1.7%	3.0%	1.8%	0.4%	0.3%	1.2%	0.1%	1.2%	1.2%
15	Netherlands	4.3%	4.0%	3.5%	1.4%	0.6%	-0.9%	1.4%	1.5%	2.5%	2.1%
16	Norway	2.6%	2.1%	-2.8%	2.7%	1.1%	0.4%	2.9%	2.5%	2.2%	2.1%
17	Poland	4.8%	4.1%	4.0%	1.0%	1.4%	3.8%	5.4%	3.4%	5.0%	5.1%
18	Portugal	4.6%	3.8%	3.4%	1.7%	0.4%	-1.1%	1.0%	0.4%	1.0%	1.4%

Sheet1 / Sheet2 / Sheet3

Ready   100%

The Row Height dialog box appears.

⑤ In the Row height text box, type the height you want to use.

⑥ Click **OK**.

● Excel adjusts the row heights.

● You can also move ✛ over the bottom edge of a row heading (✛ changes to +) and then click and drag the edge to set the height.

Simplify It

Is there an easier way to adjust the row height to fit the contents of a row?
Yes. You can use Excel's AutoFit feature, which automatically adjusts the row height to fit the tallest item in a row. Click in any cell in the row, click **Home**, click **Format**, and click **AutoFit Row Height**. Alternatively, move ✛ over the bottom edge of the row heading (✛ changes to +) and then double-click.

Is there a way to change all the row heights at once?
Yes. Click ▱ (or press Ctrl + A) to select the entire worksheet. You can then either follow the steps in this section to set the height by hand, or you can move ✛ over the bottom edge of any row heading (✛ changes to +) and then click and drag the edge to set the height of all the rows.

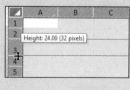

Wrap Text Within a Cell

You can make a long cell entry easier to read by wrapping the text within the cell.

If you type more text in a cell than can fit horizontally, Excel either displays the text over the next cell if that cell is empty, or Excel displays only part of the text if the next cell contains data. To prevent Excel from showing only truncated cell data, you can format the cell to wrap text within the cell. In most cases, Excel increases the row height just enough so that it can display all the text given the cell's current width.

Wrap Text Within a Cell

1 Select the cell that you want to format.

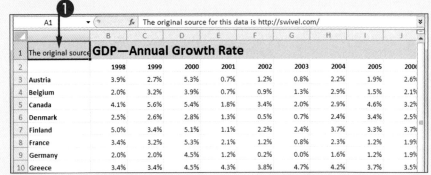

2 Click the **Home** tab.

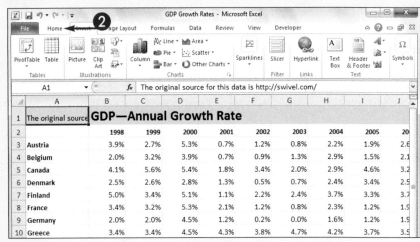

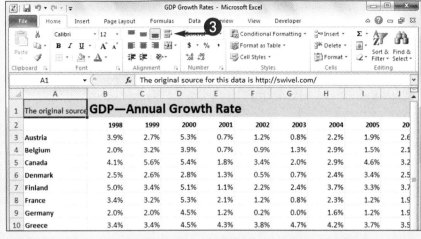

3 Click **Wrap Text** (image).

Excel turns on text wrapping for the selected cell.

- If the cell has more text than can fit horizontally, Excel wraps the text onto multiple lines and increases the row height to compensate.

Simplify It

My text is only slightly bigger than the cell. Is there a way to view the entire text without turning on text wrapping?

Yes. There are several things you can try. For example, you can widen the column until you see all your text; see "Change the Column Width" earlier in this chapter.

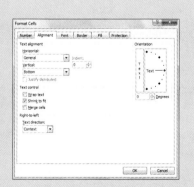

Alternatively, you can try reducing the cell font size. One way to do this is to choose a smaller value in the Font Size list of the Home tab's Font group. However, an easier way is to click the Alignment group's dialog box launcher (image) to open the Format Cells dialog box with the Alignment tab displayed. Click the **Shrink to fit** check box (image changes to image) and then click **OK**.

Add Borders to a Range

You can make a range stand out from the rest of your worksheet data by adding a border around the range. You can also use borders to make a range easier to read. For example, if your range has totals on the bottom row, you can add a double border above the totals.

Borders are also useful if a worksheet has several ranges that appear close to each other. By surrounding each range with a border, you make it clearer that your worksheet consists of multiple, separate ranges.

1 Select the range that you want to format.

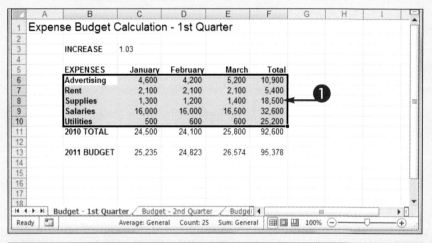

2 Click the **Home** tab.

3 Click the **Borders** ⏷.

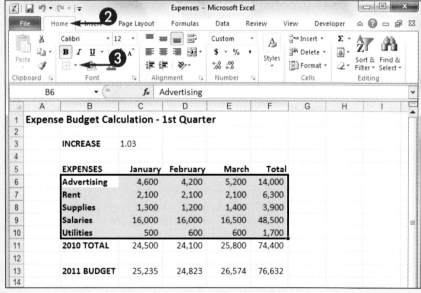

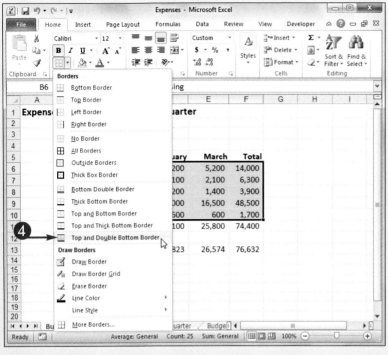

④ Click the type of border you want to use.

● Excel applies the border to the range.

How do I get my borders to stand out from the worksheet gridlines?
One way to make your borders stand out is to click the **Borders** ⋅, click **Line Style**, and then click a thicker border style. You can also click **Line Color** and then click a color that is not a shade of gray. However, perhaps the most effective method is to turn off the worksheet gridlines. Click the **View** tab, and then in the Show group click the **Gridlines** check box (☑ changes to ☐).

None of the border types is quite right for my worksheet. Can I create a custom border?
Yes. You can draw the border by hand. Click the **Borders** ⋅ and then click **Draw Border**. Use the Line Style and Line Color lists to configure your border. Click a cell edge to add a border to that edge; click and drag a range to add a border around that range. If you prefer to create a grid where the border surrounds every cell, click the **Draw Border Grid** command instead.

Chapter 6

Building Formulas and Functions

Are you ready to start creating powerful and useful worksheets by building your own formulas? This chapter explains formulas, shows you how to build them, and shows you how to incorporate Excel's versatile worksheet functions into your formulas. You also learn useful formula techniques such as how to sum a row or column of numbers, how to create quick formulas using the AutoSum feature, how to use range names and range from other workbooks in your formulas, and how to move and copy formulas.

Understanding Excel Formulas

To get the most out of Excel, you need to understand formulas so that you can perform calculations on your worksheet data. You need to know the components of a formula, you need to understand arithmetic and comparison formulas, and you need to understand the importance of precedence when building a formula.

Formulas

A *formula* is a set of symbols and values that perform some kind of calculation and produce a result. All Excel formulas have the same general structure: an equal sign (=) followed by one or more operands and operators. The equal sign tells Excel to interpret everything that follows in the cell as a formula. For example, if you type **=5+8** into a cell, Excel interprets the 5+8 text as a formula, and displays the result in the cell (13).

Operands

Every Excel formula includes one or more *operands*, which are the data that Excel uses in the calculation. The simplest type of operand is a constant value, which is usually a number. However, most Excel formulas include references to worksheet data, which can be a cell address (such as B1), a range address (such as B1:B5), or a range name. Finally, you can also use any of Excel's built-in functions as an operand.

Operators

In an Excel formula that contains two or more operands, each operand is separated by an *operator*, which is a symbol that combines the operands in some way, usually mathematically. Example operators include the plus sign (+) and the multiplication sign (*). For example, the formula =B1+B2 adds the values in cells B1 and B2.

Arithmetic Formulas

An arithmetic formula combines numeric operands — numeric constants, functions that return numeric results, and fields or items that contain numeric values — with mathematical operators to perform a calculation. Because Excel worksheets primarily deal with numeric data, arithmetic formulas are by far the most common formulas used in worksheet calculations.

There are seven arithmetic operators you can use to construct arithmetic formulas:

Operator	Name	Example	Result
+	Addition	= 10 + 5	15
–	Subtraction	= 10 – 5	5
–	Negation	= –10	–10
*	Multiplication	= 10 * 5	50
/	Division	= 10 / 5	2
%	Percentage	= 10%	0.1
^	Exponentiation	= 10 ^ 5	100000

Comparison Formulas

A comparison formula combines numeric operands — numeric constants, functions that return numeric results, and fields or items that contain numeric values — with special operators to compare one operand with another. A comparison formula always returns a logical result. This means that if the comparison is true, then the formula returns the value 1, which is equivalent to the logical value TRUE; if the comparison is false, then the formula returns the value 0, which is equivalent to the logical value FALSE.

There are six operators you can use to construct comparison formulas:

Operator	Name	Example	Result
=	Equal to	= 10 = 5	0
<	Less than	= 10 < 5	0
< =	Less than or equal to	= 10 < = 5	0
>	Greater than	= 10 > 5	1
> =	Greater than or equal to	= 10 > = 5	1
< >	Not equal to	= 10 < > 5	1

Operator Precedence

Most of your formulas include multiple operands and operators. In many cases, the order in which Excel performs the calculations is crucial. Consider the formula = 3 + 5 ^ 2. If you calculate from left to right, the answer you get is 64 (3 + 5 equals 8, and 8 ^ 2 equals 64). However, if you perform the exponentiation first and then the addition, the result is 28 (5 ^ 2 equals 25, and 3 + 25 equals 28).

To solve this problem, Excel evaluates a formula according to a predefined order of precedence, which is determined by the formula operators:

Operator	Operation	Precedence
( )	Parentheses	1st
–	Negation	2nd
%	Percentage	3rd
^	Exponentiation	4th
* and /	Multiplication and division	5th
+ and –	Addition and subtraction	6th
= < < = > > = < >	Comparison	7th

Build a Formula

You can add a formula to a worksheet cell using a technique similar to adding data to a cell. To ensure that Excel treats the text as a formula, be sure to begin with an equal sign (=) and then type your operands and operators.

When you add a formula to a cell, Excel displays the formula result in the cell, not the formula itself. For example, if you add the formula =C3+C4 to a cell, that cell displays the sum of the values in cells C3 and C4. To see the formula, click the cell and examine the Formula bar.

Build a Formula

① Click in the cell in which you want to build the formula.

② Type =.

● Your typing also appears in the Formula bar.

Note: *You can also type the formula into the Formula bar.*

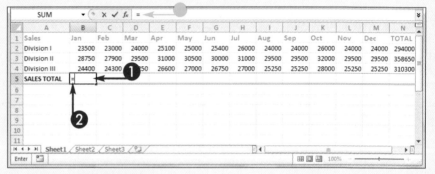

③ Type or click an operand. For example, to reference a cell in your formula, click in the cell.

● Excels inserts the address of the clicked cell into the formula.

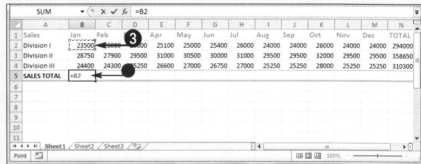

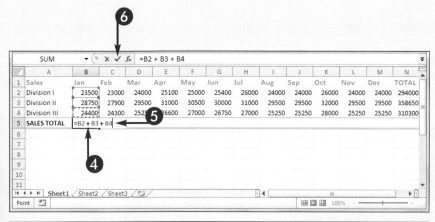

4 Type an operator.

5 Repeat Steps **3** and **4** to add other operands and operators to your formula.

6 Click ☑ or press `Enter`.

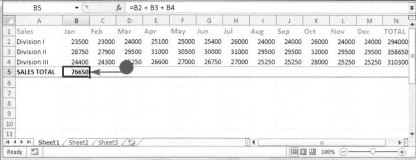

● Excel displays the formula result in the cell.

Simplify It

If Excel displays only the result of the formula, how do I make changes to the formula?
Excel displays the formula result in the cell, but it still keeps track of the original formula. To display the formula again, you have two choices: Click the cell and then edit the formula using the Formula bar, or double-click the cell to display the original formula in the cell and then edit the formula. In both cases, press `Enter` when you finish editing the formula.

If I have many formulas, is there an easy way to view the formulas?
Yes. You can configure the worksheet to show the formulas instead of their results. Click **File** and then click **Options** to open the Excel Options dialog box. Click the **Advanced** tab, scroll to the **Display options for this worksheet** section, click the **Show formulas in cells instead of their calculated results** check box (☐ changes to ☑), and then click **OK**. You can also toggle between formulas and results by pressing `Ctrl` + `` ` ``.

Understanding Excel Functions

To build powerful and useful formulas, you often need to include one or more Excel functions as operands. You need to understand the advantages of using functions, you need to know the basic structure of every function, and you need to review Excel's function types.

Functions

A *function* is a predefined formula that performs a specific task. For example, the SUM function calculates the total of a list of numbers, and the PMT (payment) function calculates a loan or mortgage payment. You can use functions on their own, preceded by =, or as part of a larger formula.

Function Advantages

Functions are designed to take you beyond the basic arithmetic and comparison formulas by offering two main advantages. First, functions make simple but cumbersome formulas easier to use. For example, calculating a loan payment requires a complex formula, but Excel's PMT function makes this easy. Second, functions enable you to include complex mathematical expressions in your worksheets that otherwise would be difficult or impossible to construct using simple arithmetic operators.

Function Structure

Every worksheet function has the same basic structure: NAME(Argument1, Argument2, ...). The NAME part identifies the function. In worksheet formulas and custom PivotTable formulas, the function name always appears in uppercase letters: PMT, SUM, AVERAGE, and so on. The items that appear within the parentheses are the functions' *arguments*. The arguments are the inputs that functions use to perform calculations. For example, the function SUM(A1,B2,C3) adds the values in cells A1, B2, and C3.

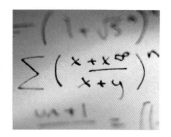

Statistical Functions

The following table lists some common statistical functions:

Function	Description
AVERAGE(number1,number2,...)	Returns the average of the arguments
COUNT(number1,number2,...)	Counts the numbers in the argument list
MAX(number1,number2,...)	Returns the maximum value of the arguments
MEDIAN(number1,number2,...)	Returns the median value of the arguments
MIN(number1,number2,...)	Returns the minimum value of the arguments
MODE(number1,number2,...)	Returns the most common value of the arguments
STDEV(number1,number2,...)	Returns the standard deviation based on a sample
STDEVP(number1,number2,...)	Returns the standard deviation based on an entire population

Financial Functions

Most of Excel's financial functions use the following arguments:

Argument	Description
rate	The fixed rate of interest over the term of the loan or investment
nper	The number of payments or deposit periods over the term of the loan or investment
pmt	The periodic payment or deposit
pv	The present value of the loan (the principal) or the initial deposit in an investment
fv	The future value of the loan or investment
type	The type of payment or deposit: 0 (the default) for end-of-period payments or deposits; 1 for beginning-of-period payments or deposits

The following table lists some common financial functions:

Function	Description
FV(rate,nper,pmt,pv,type)	Returns the future value of an investment or loan
IPMT(rate,per,nper,pv,fv,type)	Returns the interest payment for a specified period of a loan
NPER(rate,pmt,pv,fv,type)	Returns the number of periods for an investment or loan
PMT(rate,nper,pv,fv,type)	Returns the periodic payment for a loan or investment
PPMT(rate,per,nper,pv,fv,type)	Returns the principal payment for a specified period of a loan
PV(rate,nper,pmt,fv,type)	Returns the present value of an investment
RATE(nper,pmt,pv,fv,type,guess)	Returns the periodic interest rate for a loan or investment

Add a Function to a Formula

To get the benefit of an Excel function, you need to use it within a formula. You can use a function as the only operand in the formula, or you can include the function as part of a larger formula.

In "Understanding Excel Functions," you learned that Excel has many functions and that most functions take one or more arguments, but it is often difficult to remember a function's arguments and the order in which they appear. To make it easy to choose the function you need and to add the appropriate arguments, Excel offers the Insert Function feature.

Add a Function to a Formula

① Click in the cell in which you want to build the formula.

② Type **=**.

③ Type any operands and operators you need before adding the function.

④ Click the **Insert Function** button (*fx*).

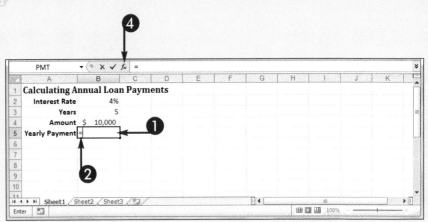

The Insert Function dialog box appears.

⑤ Click ☑ and then click the category that contains the function you want to use.

⑥ Click the function.

⑦ Click **OK**.

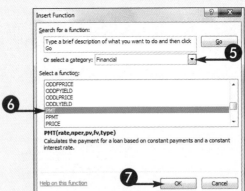

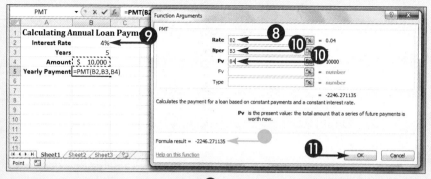

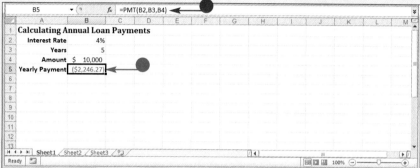

The Function Arguments dialog box appears.

⑧ Click inside an argument box.

⑨ Click the cell that contains the argument value.

You can also type the argument value.

⑩ Repeat Steps **8** and **9** to fill as many arguments as you need.

● The function result appears here.

⑪ Click **OK**.

● Excel adds the function to the formula.

● Excel displays the formula result.

Note: *In this example, the result appears in the parentheses to indicate a negative value. In loan calculations, money that you pay out is always a negative amount.*

Note: *If your formula requires any other operands and operators, press* F2 *and then type what you need to complete your formula.*

Do I have to specify a value for every function argument?

Not necessarily. Some function arguments are required to obtain a result, but some are optional. In the PMT function, for example, the rate, nper, and pv arguments are required, but the fv and type arguments are optional. When the Function Arguments dialog box displays a result for the function, then you know you have entered all of the required arguments.

How do I calculate a monthly financial result if I only have yearly values?

This is a common problem. For example, if your loan payment worksheet contains an annual interest rate and a loan term in years, how do you calculate the monthly payment using the PMT function? You need to convert the rate and term to monthly values. That is, you divide the annual interest rate by 12, and you multiply the term by 12. For example, if the annual rate is in cell B2, the term in years is in B3, and the loan amount is in B4, the function PMT(B2/12, B3*12, B4) calculates the monthly payment.

Add a Row or Column of Numbers

You can quickly add worksheet numbers by building a formula that uses Excel's SUM function.

Adding a range of numbers is probably the most common worksheet calculation, so it is useful to know how to use Excel's SUM function. Although you can use SUM to add individual cells or a rectangular range of cells, you will most often need to add a row or a column of data. In this case, when you use the SUM function in a formula, you can specify as the function's argument a reference to either a row or a column of numbers.

Add a Row or Column of Numbers

1 Click in the cell where you want the sum to appear.

2 Type **=sum(**.

● When you begin a function, Excel displays a banner that shows you the function's arguments.

Note: *In the function banner, bold arguments are required, and arguments that appear in square brackets are optional.*

3 Use the mouse ⊕ to click and drag the row or column of numbers that you want to add.

● Excel adds a reference for the range to the formula.

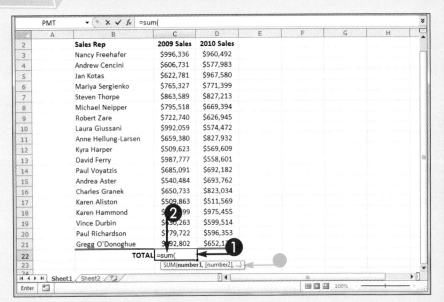

120

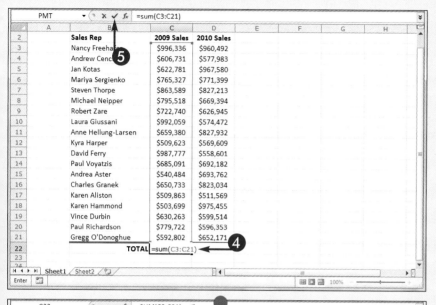

④ Type **)**.

⑤ Click ☑ or press **Enter**.

● Excel enters the formula.

● Excel displays the sum in the cell.

Can I use the SUM function to total rows and columns at the same time?
Yes, the SUM function works not only with simple row and column ranges, but with any rectangular range. After you type **=sum(**, use the mouse ⬧ to click and drag the entire range that you want to sum.

Can I use the SUM function to total only certain values in a row or column?
Yes. The SUM function can accept multiple arguments, so you can enter as many cells or ranges as you need. After you type **=sum(**, hold down **Ctrl** and either click each cell that you want to include in the total, or use the mouse ⬧ to click and drag each range that you want to sum.

Build an AutoSum Formula

You can reduce the time it takes to build a worksheet as well as reduce the possibility of errors by using Excel's AutoSum feature. By default, the AutoSum tool adds a SUM function formula to a cell and automatically adds the function arguments based on the structure of the worksheet data. However, you can also use AutoSum to quickly create simple formulas that use common functions, such as AVERAGE, COUNT, MAX, or MIN.

Build an AutoSum Formula

1 Click in the cell where you want the sum to appear.

Note: For AutoSum to work, the cell you select should be below or to the right of the range you want to sum.

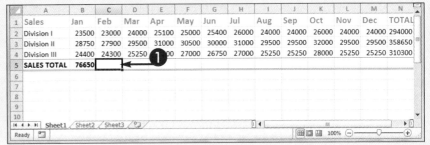

2 Click the **Sum** button (Σ).

● If you want to use a function other than SUM, click the **Sum** ⊡ and then click the operation you want to use: Average, Count Numbers, Max, or Min.

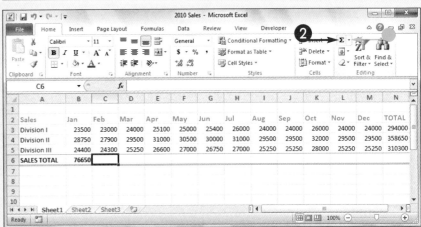

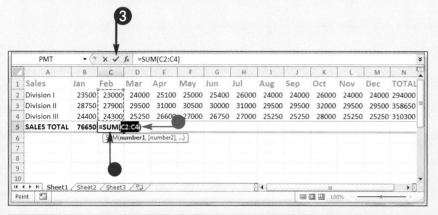

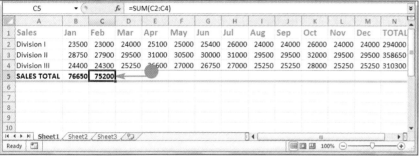

● Excel adds a SUM function formula to the cell.

   Note: *You can also press* **Alt** + **=** *instead of clicking* **Σ**.

● Excel guesses that the range above (or to the left) of the cell is the one you want to add.

   If Excel guessed wrong, select the correct range.

③ Click ☑ or press **Enter**.

● Excel displays the sum.

Simplify It

Is there a way to see the sum of a range without adding an AutoSum formula?
Yes. You can use Excel's status bar to do this. When you select any range, Excel adds the range's numeric values and displays the result on the right side of the status bar — for example, Sum: 75200. By default, Excel also displays the Average and Count. If you want to see a different calculation, right-click the result in the status bar and then click the operation you want to use: Numerical Count, Maximum, or Minimum.

Is there a faster way to add an AutoSum formula?
Yes. If you know the range you want to sum, and that range is either a vertical column with a blank cell below it or a horizontal row with a blank cell to its right, select the range (including the blank cell) and then click **Σ** or press **Alt** + **=**. Excel populates the blank cell with a SUM formula that totals the selected range.

Add a Range Name to a Formula

You can make your formulas easier to build, more accurate, and easier to read by using range names as operands. For example, the formula =SUM(B2:B10) is difficult to decipher on its own because you cannot tell at a glance what kind of data is in the range B2:B10. However, with the formula =SUM(Expenses), it is immediately obvious that the formula is adding a range of expense values.

If you are not sure what range names are or how to define a range name, see Chapter 4 to learn more about range names, including how to define names for ranges in Excel.

Add a Range Name to a Formula

① Click in the cell in which you want to build the formula, type =, and then type any operands and operators you need before adding the range name.

② Click the **Formulas** tab.

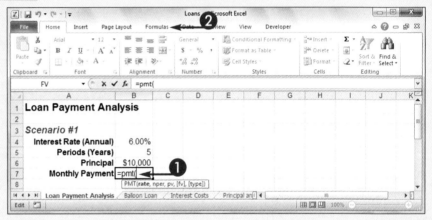

③ Click **Use in Formula**.

● Excel displays a list of the range names in the current workbook.

④ Click the range name you want to use.

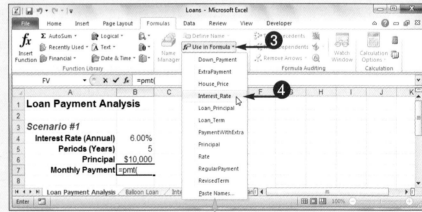

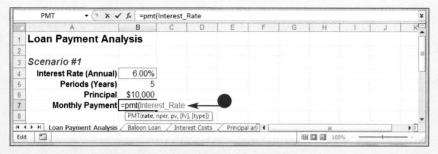

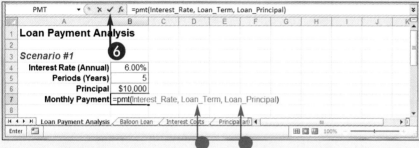

● Excel inserts the range name into the formula.

⑤ Type any operands and operators you need to complete your formula.

● If you need to insert other range names into your formula, repeat Steps **2** to **5** for each name.

⑥ Click ☑ or press Enter.

Excel calculates the formula result.

If I create a range name after I build my formula, is there an easy way to convert the range reference to the range name?
Yes. Excel offers an Apply Names feature that replaces range references with their associated range names throughout a worksheet. Click the **Formulas** tab, click the **Define Name** ⬝, and then click **Apply Names** to open the Apply Names dialog box. In the Apply names list, click the range name you want to use, and then click **OK**. Excel replaces the associated range references with the range name in each formula in the current worksheet.

Do I have to use the list of range names to insert range names into my formulas?
No. As you build your formula, you can type the range name by hand, if you know it. Alternatively, as you build your formula, click the cell or select the range that has the defined name, and Excel adds the name to your formula instead of the range address. If you want to work from a list of the defined range names, click an empty area of the worksheet, click **Formulas**, click **Use in Formula**, click **Paste Names**, and then click **Paste List**.

Reference Another Worksheet Range in a Formula

You can add flexibility to your formulas by adding references to ranges that reside in other worksheets. This enables you to take advantage of work you have done in other worksheets so you do not have to waste time repeating your work on the current worksheet.

You can even add references to ranges that reside in other workbooks, as described in the second Tip on the following page.

Reference Another Worksheet Range in a Formula

1 Click in the cell in which you want to build the formula, type **=**, and then type any operands and operators you need before adding the range reference.

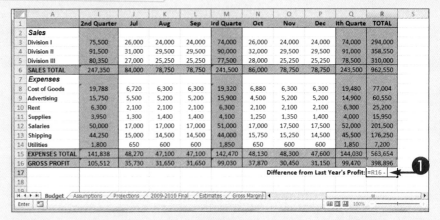

2 Press **Ctrl** + **Page down** until the worksheet you want to use appears.

126

	2nd Quarter	Jul	Aug	Sep	3rd Quarter	Oct	Nov	Dec	4th Quarter	TOTAL	
1	2nd Quarter	Jul	Aug	Sep	3rd Quarter	Oct	Nov	Dec	4th Quarter	TOTAL	
3	69,460	23,920	22,080	22,080	68,080	23,920	22,080	22,080	68,080	270,480	
4	84,180	28,520	27,140	27,140	82,800	29,440	27,140	27,140	83,720	329,866	
5	73,922	24,840	23,230	23,230	71,300	25,760	23,230	23,230	72,220	285,200	
6	227,562	77,280	72,450	72,450	222,180	79,120	72,450	72,450	224,020	885,546	
8	19,115	6,492	6,086	6,086	18,663	6,646	6,086	6,086	18,818	74,386	
9	16,538	5,775	5,460	5,460	16,695	4,725	5,460	5,460	15,645	63,578	
10	6,615	2,205	2,205	2,205	6,615	2,205	2,205	2,205	6,615	26,460	
11	4,148	1,365	1,470	1,470	4,305	1,313	1,418	1,470	4,200	16,748	
12	52,500	17,850	17,850	17,850	53,550	17,850	18,375	18,375	54,600	211,575	
13	46,463	15,750	15,225	15,225	46,200	16,538	16,013	15,225	47,775	185,063	
14	1,890	683	630	630	1,943	683	630	630	1,943	7,560	
15	147,268	50,119	48,926	48,926	147,971	49,959	50,186	49,451	149,595	585,368	
16	80,294	27,161	23,524	23,524	74,209	29,161	22,264	22,999	74,425	300,178	

Budget ... Projections | 2009-2010 Final | Estimates | Gross Margin
Point   100%

PMT   =R16 - '2009-2010 Final'!R16

	A	Jul	Aug	Sep	rd Quarte	Oct	Nov	Dec	lth Quarte	TOTAL
1		Jul	Aug	Sep	rd Quarte	Oct	Nov	Dec	lth Quarte	TOTAL
2	*Sales*									
3	Division I	26,000	24,000	24,000	74,000	26,000	24,000	24,000	74,000	294,000
4	Division II	31,000	29,500	29,500	90,000	32,000	29,500	29,500	91,000	358,550
5	Division III	27,000	25,250	25,250	77,500	28,000	25,250	25,250	78,500	310,000
6	SALES TOTAL	84,000	78,750	78,750	241,500	86,000	78,750	78,750	243,500	962,550
7	*Expenses*									
8	Cost of Goods	6,720	6,300	6,300	19,320	6,880	6,300	6,300	19,480	77,004
9	Advertising	5,500	5,200	5,200	15,900	4,500	5,200	5,200	14,900	60,550
10	Rent	2,100	2,100	2,100	6,300	2,100	2,100	2,100	6,300	25,200
11	Supplies	1,300	1,400	1,400	4,100	1,250	1,350	1,400	4,000	15,950
12	Salaries	17,000	17,000	17,000	51,000	17,000	17,500	17,500	52,000	201,500
13	Shipping	15,000	14,500	14,500	44,000	15,750	15,250	14,500	45,500	176,250
14	Utilities	650	600	600	1,850	650	600	600	1,850	7,200
15	EXPENSES TOTAL	48,270	47,100	47,100	142,470	48,130	48,300	47,600	144,030	563,654
16	GROSS PROFIT	35,730	31,650	31,650	99,030	37,870	30,450	31,150	99,470	398,896
17					Difference from Last Year's Profit:	=R16 - '2009-2010 Final'!R16				

Budget | Assumptions | Projections | 2009-2010 Final | Estimates | Gross Margin
Point   100%

❸ Select the range you want to use.

❹ Press Ctrl + Page up until you return to the original worksheet.

● A reference to the range on the other worksheet appears in your formula.

❺ Type any operands and operators you need to complete your formula.

❻ Click ☑ or press Enter.

Excel calculates the formula result.

Simplify It

Can I reference a range in another worksheet by hand?
Yes. Rather than selecting the other worksheet range with your mouse, you can type the range reference directly into your formula. Type the worksheet name, surrounded by single quotation marks (') if the name contains a space; type an exclamation mark (!); then type the cell or range address. Here is an example: **'Expenses 2010'!B2:B10**.

Can I reference a range in another workbook in my formula?
Yes. First make sure the workbook you want to reference is open. When you reach the point in your formula where you want to add the reference, click the Excel icon (🗐) in the Windows taskbar, and then click the other workbook to switch to it. Click the worksheet that has the range you want to reference, and then select the range. Click 🗐 and then click the original workbook to switch back to it. Excel adds the other workbook range reference to your formula.

Move or Copy a Formula

You can restructure or reorganize a worksheet by moving an existing formula to a different part of the worksheet. When you move a formula, Excel preserves the formula's range references.

Excel also enables you to make a copy of a formula, which is a useful technique if you require a duplicate of the formula elsewhere or if you require a formula that is similar to an existing formula. When you copy a formula, Excel adjusts the range references to the new location.

Move or Copy a Formula

Move a Formula

1 Click the cell that contains the formula you want to move.

2 Position ⟳ over any outside border of the cell.

⟳ changes to ⬉.

3 Click and drag the cell to the new location.

⬉ changes to ⬉.

● Excel displays an outline of the cell.

● Excel displays the address of the new location.

4 Release the mouse button.

● Excel moves the formula to the new location.

● Excel does not change the formula's range references.

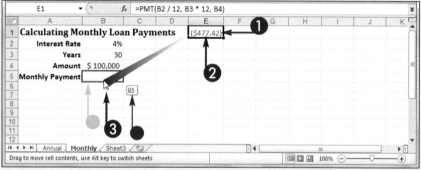

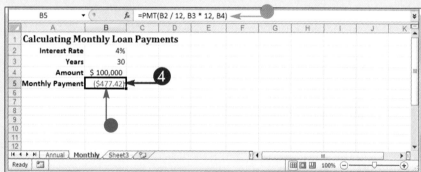

128

CHAPTER 6

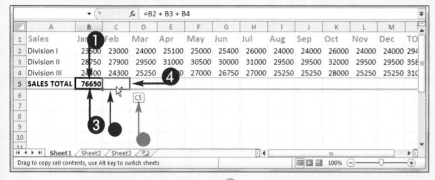

Copy a Formula

1️⃣ Click the cell that contains the formula you want to copy.

2️⃣ Press and hold Ctrl.

3️⃣ Position ✥ over any outside border of the cell.

✥ changes to ↖.

4️⃣ Click and drag the cell to the location where you want the copy to appear.

● Excel displays an outline of the cell.

● Excel displays the address of the new location.

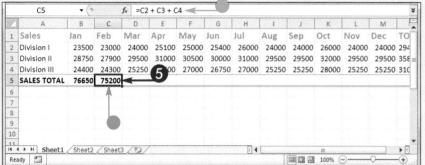

5️⃣ Release the mouse button.

6️⃣ Release Ctrl.

● Excel creates a copy of the formula in the new location.

● Excel adjusts the range references.

Note: *You can make multiple copies by dragging the bottom-right corner of the cell. Excel fills the adjacent cells with copies of the formula.*

Why does Excel adjust the range references when I copy a formula?
When you make a copy of a formula, Excel assumes that you want that copy to reference different ranges than in the original formula. In particular, Excel assumes that the ranges you want to use in the new formula are positioned relative to the ranges used in the original formula, and that the relative difference is equal to the number of rows and columns you dragged the cell to create the copy.

For example, suppose your original formula references cell A1, and you make a copy of the formula in the cell one column to the right. In that case, Excel also adjusts the cell reference one column to the right, so it becomes B1 in the new formula.

If you do not want Excel to adjust a range reference, switch the reference to the absolute format. Double-click the cell that contains the formula you want to edit, select the cell reference you want to change, and then press F4.

Chapter 7

Manipulating Excel Worksheets

An Excel worksheet is where you enter your headings and data and build your formulas. You will spend most of your time in Excel operating within a worksheet, so you need to know how to navigate a worksheet as well as how to perform useful worksheet tasks, such as renaming worksheets; creating new worksheets; and moving, copying, and deleting worksheets. In this chapter you also learn how to change the gridline color, and how to toggle gridlines and headings on and off.

	97,000	137,000	13,5
	78,000	140,000	13,5
	48,778	89,678	13,5
	76,551	117,451	13,5
	33,737	74,637	13,5
	29,500	70,400	13,5
	43,115	84,015	13,5
	63,991	104,891	13,5
	20,377	61,777	13,5

Navigate a Worksheet

You can use a few keyboard techniques that make it easier to navigate data after it is entered in a worksheet.

After you enter data into a cell, it is usually easiest to use your mouse to click in the next cell you want to work with. However, if you are entering data and your hands are already on the keyboard, then it is often faster to use the keyboard to navigate to the next cell.

Keyboard Techniques for Navigating a Worksheet	
Press	**To Move**
←	Left one cell
→	Right one cell
↑	Up one cell
↓	Down one cell
Home	To the beginning of the current row
Page down	Down one screen
Page up	Up one screen
Alt + Page down	One screen to the right
Alt + Page up	One screen to the left
Ctrl + Home	To the beginning of the worksheet
Ctrl + End	To the bottom right corner of the used portion of the worksheet
Ctrl + arrow keys	In the direction of the arrow to the next non-blank cell if the current cell is blank, or to the last non-blank cell if the current cell is not blank

Rename a Worksheet

You can make your Excel workbooks easier to understand and navigate by providing each worksheet with a name that reflects the contents of the sheet.

Excel provides worksheets with generic names such as Sheet1 and Sheet2, but you can change these to more descriptive names such as Sales 2010, Amortization, or Budget Data. You can use any combination of letters, numbers, and symbols in a worksheet name, but the maximum number of characters you can use in the name is 31.

Rename a Worksheet

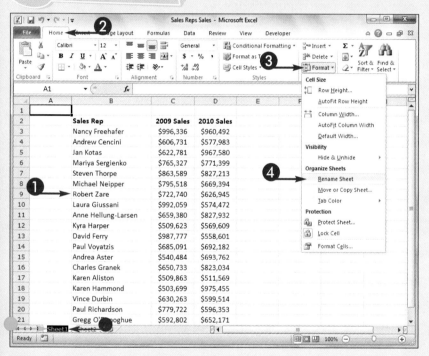

❶ Display the worksheet you want to rename.

❷ Click the **Home** tab.

❸ Click **Format**.

❹ Click **Rename Sheet**.

⬤ You can also double-click the worksheet's tab.

⬤ Excel opens the worksheet name for editing and selects the text.

❺ If you want to edit the existing name, press either ◄ or ► to deselect the text.

❻ Type the new worksheet name.

❼ Press Enter.

Excel assigns the new name to the worksheet.

Create a New Worksheet

Excel supports multiple worksheets in a single workbook, so you can add as many worksheets as you need for your project or model.

Each new Excel workbook comes with three worksheets, but it is not uncommon to require four or more worksheets in a workbook. In most cases, you will add a blank worksheet, but Excel also comes with several predefined worksheet templates that you can use. Note that there is no practical limit to the number of worksheets you can add to a workbook.

Create a New Worksheet

Insert a Blank Worksheet

1. Open the workbook to which you want to add the worksheet.

2. Click the **Home** tab.

3. Click the **Insert** ⊡.

4. Click **Insert Sheet**.

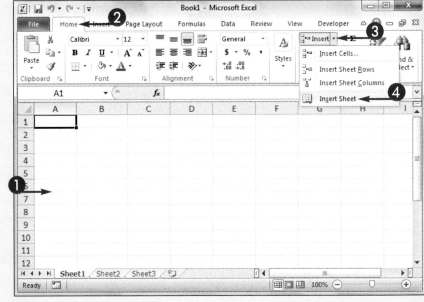

● Excel inserts the worksheet.

> **Note:** You can also insert a blank worksheet by pressing `Shift` + `F11`.

> **Note:** You can also create a new worksheet by clicking the **Insert Worksheet** button (⊡).

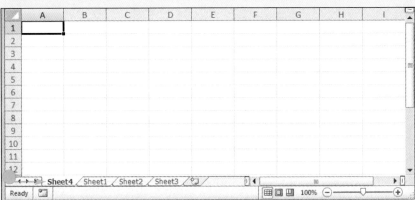

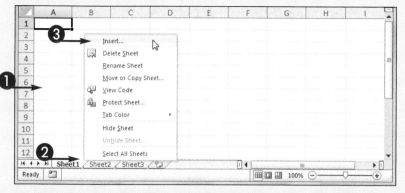

Insert a Worksheet from a Template

1 Open the workbook to which you want to add the worksheet.

2 Right-click a worksheet tab.

3 Click **Insert**.

The Insert dialog box appears.

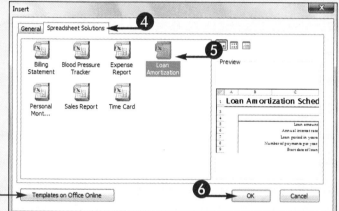

4 Click the **Spreadsheet Solutions** tab.

5 Click the type of worksheet you want to add.

● You can also click **Templates on Office Online** to download worksheet templates from the Web.

6 Click **OK**.

● Excel inserts the worksheet.

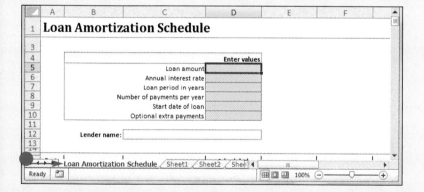

How do I navigate from one worksheet to another?
Click the tab of the worksheet you want to use. Press
`Ctrl` + `Page down` to move to the next worksheet, and
`Ctrl` + `Page up` to move to the previous worksheet.
You can also click the following controls:

◄	Move to the first worksheet.
◄	Move to the previous worksheet.
►	Move to the next worksheet.
►	Move to the last worksheet.

Move a Worksheet

You can organize an Excel workbook and make it easier to navigate by moving your worksheets to different positions within the workbook.

Although you will most often move a worksheet to a different position within the same workbook, it is also possible to move a worksheet to another workbook.

Move a Worksheet

1 If you want to move the worksheet to another workbook, open that workbook and then return to the current workbook.

2 Click the tab of the worksheet you want to move.

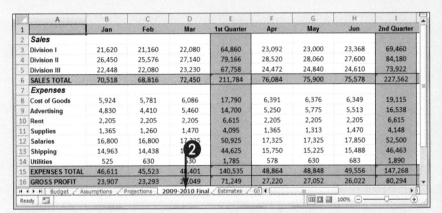

3 Click the **Home** tab.

4 Click **Format**.

5 Click **Move or Copy Sheet**.

● You can also right-click the tab and then click **Move or Copy Sheet**.

The Move or Copy dialog box appears.

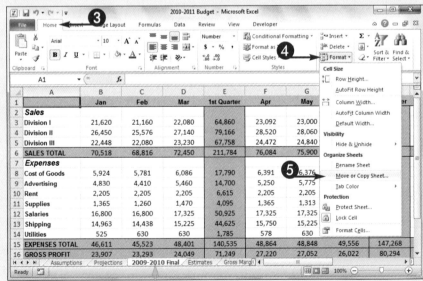

	A	B	C	D	E	F	G	H	I
1		Jan	Feb	Mar	1st Quarter	Apr	May	Jun	2nd Quarter
2	*Sales*								
3	Division I	21,620	21,160	22,080	64,860	23,092	23,000	23,368	69,460
4	Division II	26,450	25,576	27,140	79,166	28,520	28,060	27,600	84,180
5	Division III	22,448	22,080	23,230	67,758	24,472	24,840	24,610	73,922
6	SALES TOTAL	70,518	68,816	72,450	211,784	76,084	75,900	75,578	227,562
7	*Expenses*								
8	Cost of Goods	5,924	5,781	6,086	17,790	6,391	6,376	6,349	19,115
9	Advertising	4,830	4,410	5,460	14,700	5,250	5,775	5,513	16,538
10	Rent	2,205	2,205	2,205	6,615	2,205	2,205	2,205	6,615
11	Supplies	1,365	1,260	1,470	4,095	1,365	1,313	1,470	4,148
12	Salaries	16,800	16,800	17,325	50,925	17,325	17,325	17,850	52,500
13	Shipping	14,963	14,438	15,225	44,625	15,750	15,225	15,488	46,463
14	Utilities	525	630	630	1,785	578	630	683	1,890
15	EXPENSES TOTAL	46,611	45,523	48,401	140,535	48,864	48,848	49,556	147,268
16	GROSS PROFIT	23,907	23,293	24,049	71,249	27,220	27,052	26,022	80,294

⑥ If you want to move the sheet to another workbook, click the **To book** ⏷ and then click the workbook.

⑦ Use the Before sheet list to click a destination worksheet.

When Excel moves the worksheet, it will appear to the left of the sheet you selected in Step **7**.

⑧ Click **OK**.

● Excel moves the worksheet.

Simplify It

Is there an easier way to move a worksheet within the same workbook?
Yes. It is usually much easier to use your mouse to move a worksheet within the same workbook:

① Move ▷ over the tab of the worksheet you want to move.

② Click and drag the worksheet tab left or right to the new position within the workbook.

▷ changes to ▷.

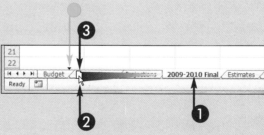

● As you drag, an arrow shows the position of the worksheet.

③ When you have the worksheet positioned where you want it, drop the worksheet tab.

Excel moves the worksheet.

Copy a Worksheet

Excel enables you to make a copy of a worksheet, which is a useful technique if you require a new worksheet that is similar to an existing worksheet. Rather than re-creating the new worksheet from scratch, you can make a copy of an existing worksheet and then edit the copy as needed.

Although you will most often copy a worksheet within the same workbook, it is also possible to copy the worksheet to another workbook.

Copy a Worksheet

1 If you want to copy the worksheet to another workbook, open that workbook and then return to the current workbook.

2 Click the tab of the worksheet you want to copy.

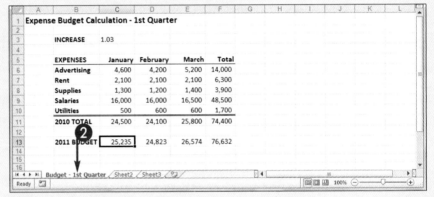

3 Click the **Home** tab.

4 Click **Format**.

5 Click **Move or Copy Sheet**.

● You can also right-click the tab and then click **Move or Copy Sheet**.

The Move or Copy dialog box appears.

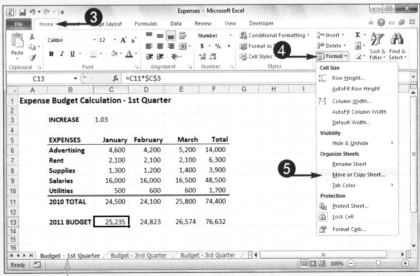

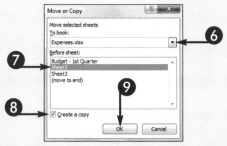

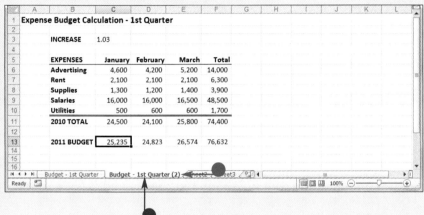

6 If you want to copy the sheet to another workbook, click the **To book** ☐ and then click the workbook.

7 Use the Before sheet list to click a destination worksheet.

When Excel copies the worksheet, the copy will appear to the left of the sheet you selected in Step **7.**

8 Click the **Create a copy** check box (☐ changes to ☑).

9 Click **OK**.

● Excel copies the worksheet.

● Excel gives the new worksheet the same name as the original, but with (2) appended.

Note: *See "Rename a Worksheet" earlier in this chapter to learn how to edit the name of the copied worksheet.*

Is there an easier way to copy a worksheet within the same workbook?
Yes. It is usually much easier to use your mouse to copy a worksheet within the same workbook:

1 Move ▹ over the tab of the worksheet you want to copy.

2 Hold down Ctrl.

3 Click and drag the worksheet tab left or right.

▹ changes to ▹.

● As you drag, an arrow shows the position of the worksheet.

4 When you have the worksheet positioned where you want it, drop the worksheet tab.

Excel copies the worksheet.

Delete a Worksheet

If you have a worksheet that you no longer need, you can delete it from the workbook. This reduces the size of the workbook, reduces clutter in the worksheet tabs, and makes the workbook easier to navigate.

It is important to note that you cannot undo a worksheet deletion. Therefore, it is always a good practice to check the worksheet contents carefully before proceeding with the deletion. If the worksheet contains any data you need but you still want to remove the worksheet, cut or copy the data and paste it into another worksheet.

Delete a Worksheet

① Click the tab of the worksheet you want to delete.

② Click the **Home** tab.

③ Click the **Delete** ⊡.

④ Click **Delete Sheet**.

● You can also right-click the tab and then click **Delete Sheet**.

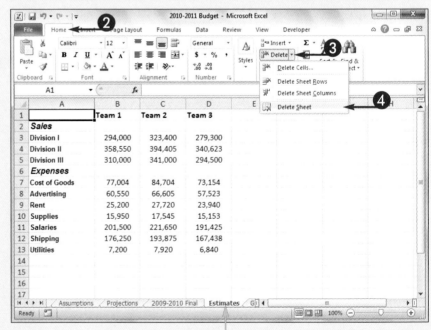

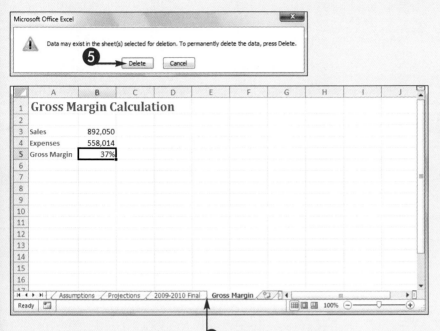

If the worksheet contains data, Excel asks you to confirm that you want to delete the worksheet.

⑤ Click **Delete**.

● Excel removes the worksheet.

I have several worksheets I need to delete. Do I have to delete them individually?
No. You can select all the sheets you want to remove and then run the deletion. To select multiple worksheets, click the tab of one of the worksheets, hold down `Ctrl`, and then click the tabs of the other worksheets.

If your workbook has many worksheets and you want to delete most of them, an easy way to select the sheets is to right-click any worksheet tab and then click **Select All Sheets**. Hold down `Ctrl`, and then click the tabs of the worksheets that you do not want to delete.

After you have selected your worksheets, follow Steps **3** to **5** to delete all the selected worksheets at once.

Change the Gridline Color

You can add some visual interest to your worksheet by changing the color that Excel uses to display the gridlines. The default color is blank, but Excel offers a palette of 56 colors that you can choose from.

Changing the gridline color also has practical value because it enables you to differentiate between the gridlines and the borders that you add to a range or a table.

Change the Gridline Color

① Click the tab of the worksheet you want to customize.

② Click the **File** tab.

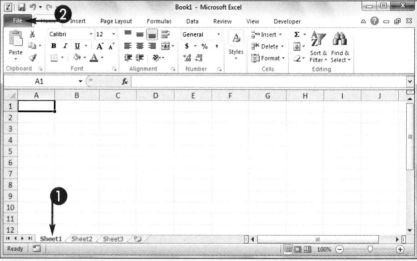

③ Click **Options**.

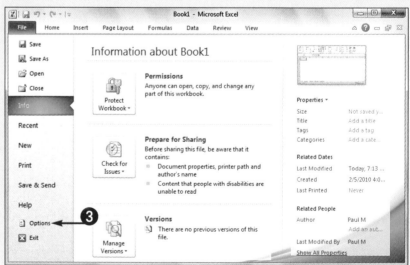

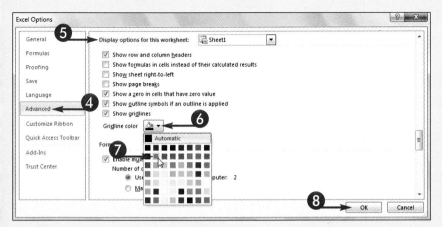

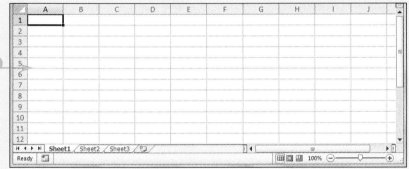

The Excel Options dialog box appears.

④ Click **Advanced**.

⑤ Scroll down to the Display options for this worksheet section.

⑥ Click the **Gridline color** 🔽.

⑦ Click the color you want to use.

⑧ Click **OK**.

● Excel displays the gridlines using the color you selected.

Simplify It

Can I change the gridline color for all the sheets in my workbook?
Yes. One method would be to follow the steps in this section for each worksheet in your workbook. However, an easier method is to first select all the sheets in the workbook. To do this, right-click any worksheet tab and then click **Select All Sheets**.

You can now follow Steps **2** to **8** to apply the new gridline color to all your worksheets. Once you have done that, right-click any worksheet tab and then click **Ungroup Sheets** to collapse the grouping.

Toggle Worksheet Gridlines On and Off

You can make your worksheet look cleaner and make the worksheet text easier to read by turning off the sheet gridlines. When you do this, Excel displays the worksheet with a plain white background, which often makes the worksheet easier to read.

If you find you have trouble selecting ranges with the gridlines turned off, you can easily turn them back on again.

Toggle Worksheet Gridlines On and Off

Turn Gridlines Off

1 Click the tab of the worksheet you want to work with.

2 Click the **View** tab.

3 Click **Gridlines** (☑ changes to ☐).

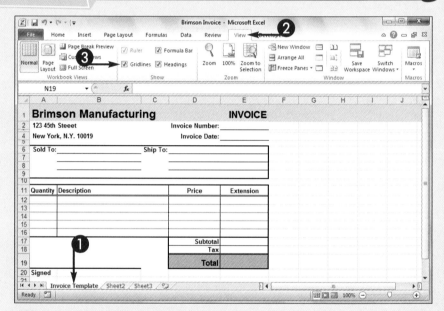

● Excel turns off the gridline display.

Turn Gridlines On

● To turn the gridlines back on, click **Gridlines** (☐ changes to ☑).

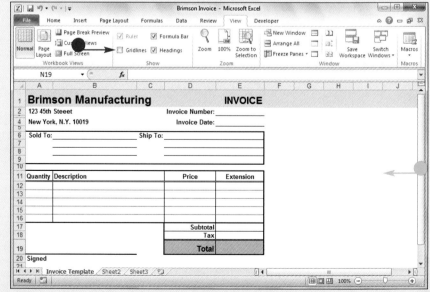

Toggle Worksheet Headings On and Off

You can give yourself a bit more room to work by turning off the worksheet's row headings — the numbers 1, 2, and so on to the left of the worksheet — and column headings — the letters A, B, and so on above the worksheet.

If you find you have trouble reading your worksheet or building formulas with the headings turned off, you can easily turn them back on again.

Toggle Worksheet Headings On and Off

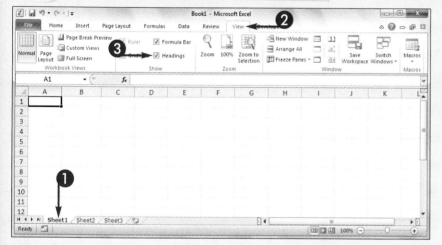

Turn Headings Off

① Click the tab of the worksheet you want to work with.

② Click the **View** tab.

③ Click **Headings** (☑ changes to ☐).

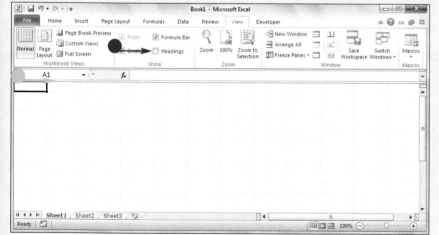

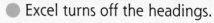

● Excel turns off the headings.

Turn Headings On

● To turn the headings back on, click **Headings** (☐ changes to ☑).

Chapter 8

Dealing with Excel Workbooks

Everything you do in Excel takes place within a *workbook*, which is the standard Excel file. This chapter shows you how to get more out of workbooks by creating new workbooks, either blank or from a template; saving and opening workbooks; arranging workbooks within the Excel window; and finding and replacing text within a workbook.

Create a New Blank Workbook

To perform new work in Excel, you need to first create a new, blank Excel workbook. Excel automatically creates a blank workbook each time you start the program, but for subsequent files you must create a new workbook yourself.

If you prefer to create a workbook based on one of Excel's templates, see "Create a New Workbook from a Template."

Create a New Blank Workbook

1 Click the **File** tab.

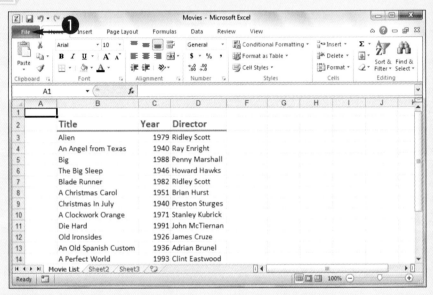

2 Click **New**.

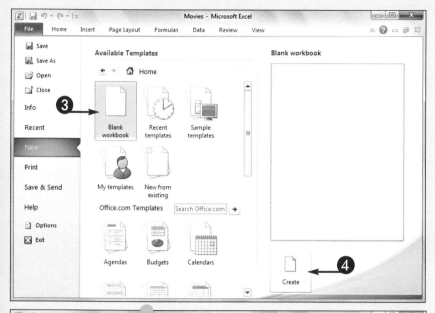

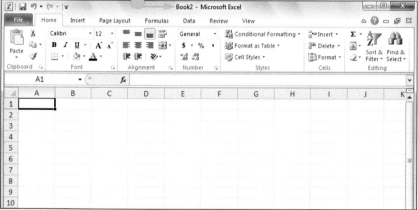

3 Click **Blank Workbook**.

4 Click **Create**.

● Excel creates the blank workbook and displays it in the Excel window.

Is there a faster method I can use to create a new workbook?
Yes. Excel offers a keyboard shortcut for faster workbook creation. From the keyboard, press Ctrl + N.

When I start Excel and then open an existing workbook, Excel often removes the new, blank workbook that it opened automatically. How can I prevent this?
Excel assumes that you want to use a fresh workbook when you start the program, so it opens a blank workbook for you automatically. However, if you do not make any changes to the blank workbook and then open an existing file, Excel assumes you do not want to use the new workbook, so it closes it. To prevent this from happening, make a change to the blank workbook before opening any existing file.

Create a New Workbook from a Template

You can save time and effort by creating a new workbook based on one of Excel's template files. Each template includes a working spreadsheet model that includes predefined labels and formulas, as well as preformatted colors, fonts, styles, and more.

Excel 2010 offers seven templates, including Expense Report, Loan Amortization, and Personal Monthly Budget. However, there are many more templates available through Microsoft Office Online.

Create a New Workbook from a Template

1 Click the **File** tab.

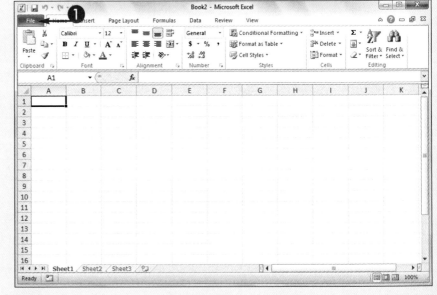

2 Click **New**.

3 Click **Sample templates**.

● To use an Office Online template, click a category in the Office.com Templates section. Click the template you want to use, and then click **Download**.

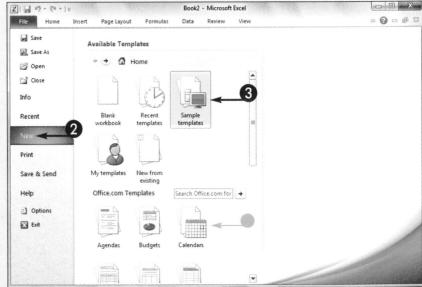

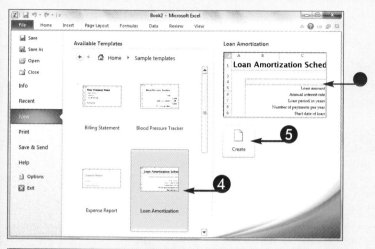

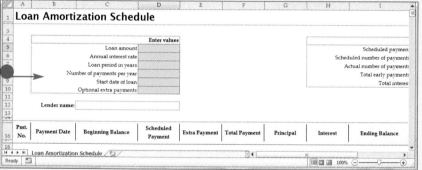

④ Click the template you want to use.

● A preview of the template appears here.

⑤ Click **Create**.

● Excel creates the new workbook and displays it in the Excel window.

Can I create my own template?
Yes. If you have a specific workbook structure that you use frequently, you should save it as a template so that you do not have to re-create the same structure from scratch each time. Open the workbook, click **File**, and then click **Save As**. In the Save As dialog box, click the **Save as type** ▾ and then click **Excel Template**. Type a **File name** and then click **Save**. To use the template, click **File**, click **New**, and then click **My Templates**.

Can I create a new workbook based on an existing workbook?
Yes. This is useful if you want to create a new workbook that is the same or similar to an existing file. Click **File**, click **New**, and then click **New from Existing**. In the New from Existing Workbook dialog box, click the existing workbook and then click **Open**.

Save a Workbook

After you create a workbook in Excel and make changes to it, you can save the document to preserve your work.

When you edit a workbook, Excel stores the changes in your computer's memory, which is erased each time you shut down your computer. Saving the document preserves your changes on your computer's hard drive, so to avoid losing your work, you should save a workbook as often as is practical.

Save a Workbook

1 Click the **File** tab.

2 Click **Save** (🖫).

You can also click 🖫 in the Quick Access Toolbar, or you can press Ctrl + S.

If you have saved the document previously, your changes are now preserved, and you can skip the rest of these steps.

The Save As dialog box appears.

If this is a new document that you have never saved before, the Save dialog box appears.

3 Click in the **File name** text box and type the name that you want to use for the document.

4 Select a folder in which to store the file.

5 Click **Save**.

Excel saves the file.

Note: *To learn how to save a workbook in an older Excel format, see Chapter 13.*

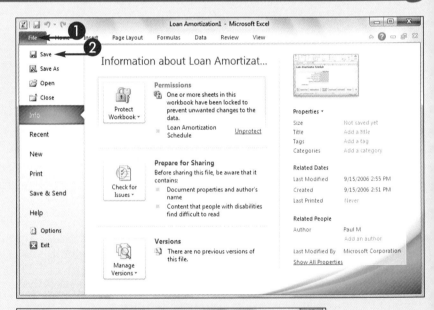

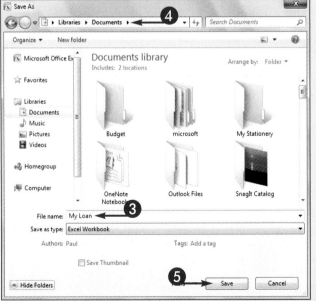

Open a Workbook

To view or make changes to an Excel workbook that you have saved in the past, you can open the workbook in Excel.

If you have used the workbook recently, you can save time by opening the workbook from Excel's Recent menu, which displays the most recent 22 files you worked with in Excel.

Open a Workbook

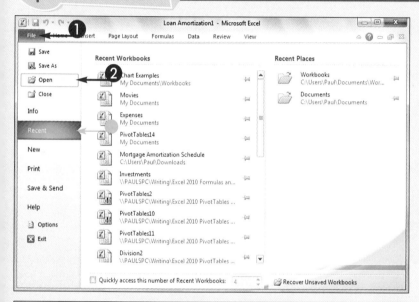

① Click the **File** tab.

● You can click **Recent** to see a list of your recently used workbooks. If you see the file you want, click it and then skip the rest of these steps.

② Click **Open** (⬚).

You can also press Ctrl + O.

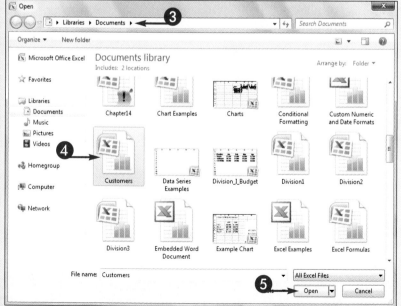

The Open dialog box appears.

③ Select the folder that contains the workbook you want to open.

④ Click the workbook.

⑤ Click **Open**.

The workbook appears in a window.

Arrange Workbook Windows

You can view two or more workbooks at once by arranging the workbook windows within the main Excel window. This enables you to easily compare the contents of the workbooks. Arranging workbook windows also enables you to more easily copy or move data among workbooks.

Excel offers four view modes for arranging workbook windows: Tiled, Horizontal, Vertical, and Cascade.

Arrange Workbook Windows

1 Open the workbooks you want to view.

2 Click the **View** tab.

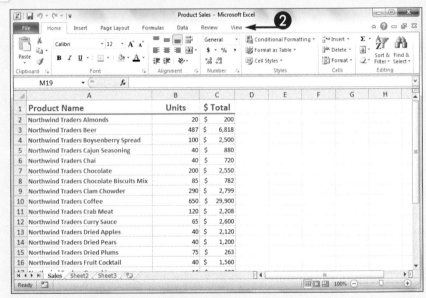

3 Click **Arrange All** (▤).

The Arrange Windows dialog box appears.

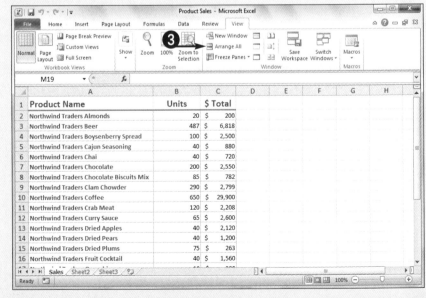

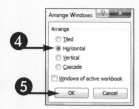

④

⑤

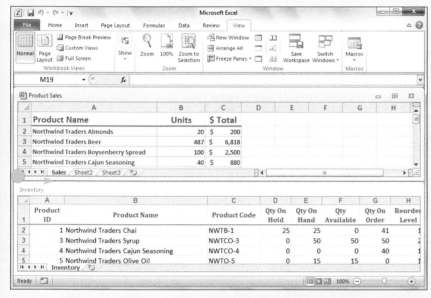

④ Click a view mode (◎ changes to ⦿).

Tiled arranges the workbooks evenly within the Excel window.

Horizontal stacks the workbooks one above the other.

Vertical displays the workbooks side by side.

Cascade arranges the workbooks in an overlapping cascade pattern.

⑤ Click **OK**.

● Excel arranges the workbook windows.

This example shows two workbooks arranged with the Horizontal view mode.

How do I return to viewing one workbook at a time?
Click the workbook you want to use, and then click the workbook window's **Maximize** button (▣). This maximizes the workbook within the Excel window, so you only see that workbook. Excel also maximizes the other open workbooks, but you only see them if you switch to them.

Is it possible to view two different sections of a single workbook at the same time?
Yes. Excel enables you to create a second window for a workbook, and you can then arrange the two windows as described in this section. To create the second window, switch to the workbook you want to view, click the **View** tab, and then click **New Window** (▤). Follow Steps **1** to **4** to open the Arrange Windows dialog box and select a view option. Click the **Windows of active workbook** check box (▢ changes to ☑), and then click **OK**.

Find Text in a Workbook

If you need to find specific text in a workbook, you can save a lot of time by using Excel's Find feature, which searches the entire workbook in the blink of an eye.

In a workbook that has only a small amount of data and just a few worksheets, you can usually find the data you want fairly quickly. However, in a large workbook with multiple sheets, it can be time-consuming to find specific text, so Excel's Find feature can help.

Find Text in a Workbook

① Click the **Home** tab.

② Click **Find & Select**.

③ Click **Find**.

Note: *You can also run the Find command by pressing* <kbd>Ctrl</kbd> + <kbd>F</kbd>.

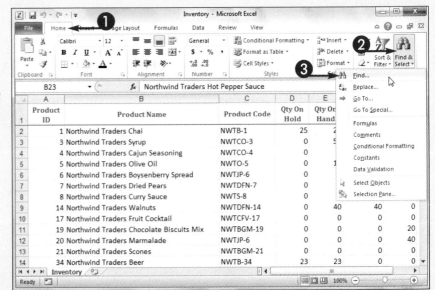

The Find and Replace dialog box appears.

④ Click in the **Find what** text box and type the text you want to find.

⑤ Click **Find Next**.

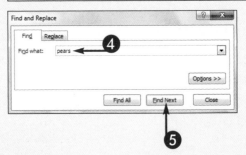

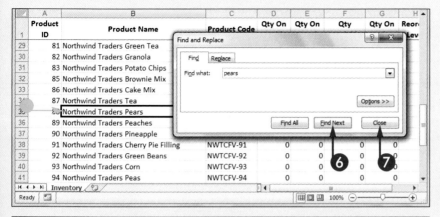

Excel selects the next cell that contains an instance of the search text.

Note: If the search text does not exist in the document, Excel displays a dialog box to let you know.

6 If the selected instance is not the one you want, click **Find Next** until Excel finds the correct instance.

7 Click **Close** to close the Find and Replace dialog box.

● Excel leaves the cell selected.

When I search for a particular term, Excel only looks in the current worksheet. How can I get Excel to search the entire workbook?
In Excel's Find and Replace dialog box, click **Options** to expand the dialog box. Click the **Within** ☐ and then click **Workbook**. This option tells Excel to examine the entire workbook for your search text.

When I search for a name such as Bill, Excel also matches the non-name bill. Is there a way to fix this?
In Excel's Find and Replace dialog box, click **Options** to expand the dialog box. Select the **Match case** check box (☐ changes to ☑). This option tells Excel to match the search text only if it has the same mix of uppercase and lowercase letters that you specify in the Find what text box. If you type **Bill**, for example, the program matches only *Bill* and not *bill*.

Replace Text in a Workbook

With Excel's Replace feature, you can quickly and easily substitute one bit of text with another throughout a workbook.

Do you need to replace a word or part of a word with some other text? If you have several instances to replace, you can save time and do a more accurate job if you let Excel's Replace feature substitute the text for you.

Replace Text in a Workbook

1 Click the **Home** tab.

2 Click **Find & Select**.

3 Click **Replace**.

> **Note:** You can also run the Replace command by pressing `Ctrl` + `H`.

The Find and Replace dialog box appears.

4 In the Find what text box, type the text you want to find.

5 In the Replace with text box, type the text you want to use as the replacement.

6 Click **Find Next**.

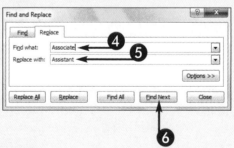

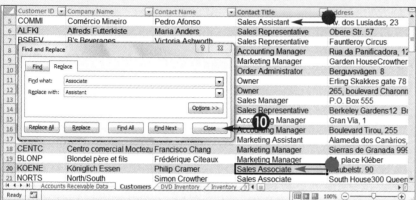

● Excel selects the cell that contains the next instance of the search text.

Note: *If the search text does not exist in the document, Excel displays a dialog box to let you know.*

7 If the selected instance is not the one you want, click **Find Next** until Excel finds the correct instance.

8 Click **Replace**.

● Excel replaces the selected text with the replacement text.

● Excel selects the next instance of the search text.

9 Repeat Steps **7** and **8** until you have replaced all of the instances you want to replace.

10 Click **Close** to close the Find and Replace dialog box.

Is there a faster way to replace every instance of the search text with the replacement text?
Yes. In the Find and Replace dialog box, click **Replace All**. This tells Excel to replace every instance of the search text with the replacement text. However, you should exercise some caution with this feature because it may make some replacements that you did not intend. Click **Find Next** a few times to make sure the matches are correct. Also, consider clicking **Options** and then selecting the **Match case** check box (☐ changes to ☑), as described in "Find Text in a Workbook."

Chapter 9

Formatting Excel Workbooks

Excel offers several settings that enable you to control the look of a workbook. These include the workbook colors for things like text and borders; fonts that govern the look of headings and regular cell text; and special effects that you can apply to charts and graphic objects. You can also format workbook colors, fonts, and effects all at once by applying a workbook theme.

Modify the Workbook Colors

You can give your workbook a new look by selecting a different color scheme. Each color scheme affects the workbook's text colors, background colors, border colors, and more. Excel offers more than 20 color schemes.

To get the most out of Excel's color schemes, you must apply styles to your ranges, as described in Chapter 5.

Modify the Workbook Colors

① Open or switch to the workbook you want to format.

② Click the **Page Layout** tab.

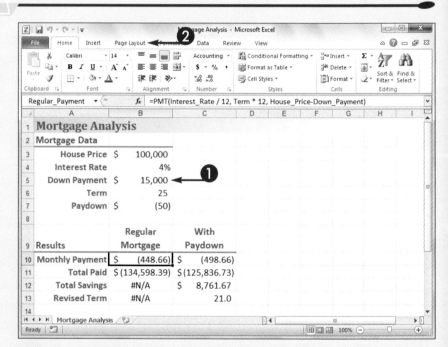

③ Click **Colors** (🔲).

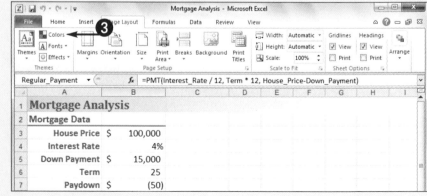

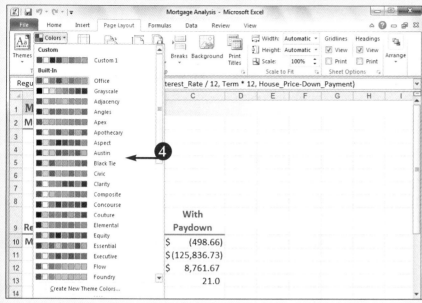

④ Click the color scheme you want to apply.

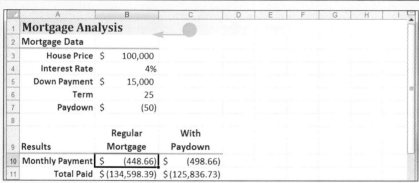

● Excel applies the color scheme to the workbook.

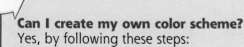

Can I create my own color scheme?
Yes, by following these steps:

❶ Click the **Page Layout** tab.

❷ Click 🔲.

❸ Click **Create New Theme Colors**.

❹ For each theme color, click 🔽 and then click the color you want to use.

● The Sample area shows what your theme colors look like.

❺ Type a name for the custom color scheme.

❻ Click **Save**.

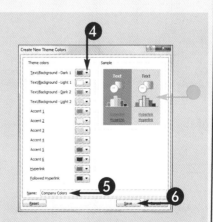

Set the Workbook Fonts

You can add visual appeal to your workbook by selecting a different font scheme. Each font scheme has two defined fonts: a *heading font* for the titles and headings, and a *body font* for the regular worksheet text. Excel offers more than 20 font schemes.

To get the most out of Excel's font schemes, particularly the heading fonts, you must apply styles to your ranges, as described in Chapter 5.

Set the Workbook Fonts

1 Open or switch to the workbook you want to format.

2 Click the **Page Layout** tab.

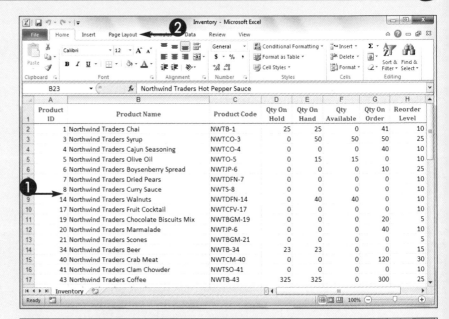

3 Click **Fonts** (A).

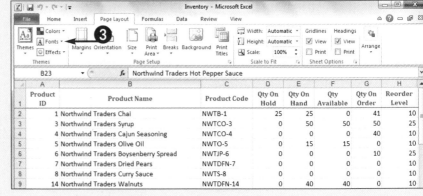

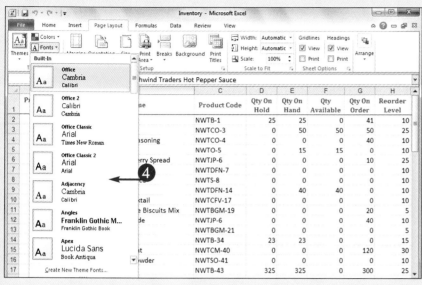

④ Click the font scheme you want to apply.

● Excel applies the heading font to the workbook's headings.

● Excel applies the body font to the workbook's regular text.

Simplify It

Can I create my own font scheme?
Yes, by following these steps:

❶ Click the **Page Layout** tab.

❷ Click Ⓐ.

❸ Click **Create New Theme Fonts**.

❹ Click the **Heading font** ⊡ and then click the font you want to use for titles and headings.

❺ Click the **Body font** ⊡ and then click the font you want to use for regular sheet text.

● The Sample area shows what your theme fonts look like.

❻ Type a name for the custom font scheme.

❼ Click **Save**.

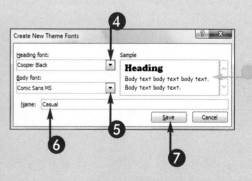

Choose Workbook Effects

You can enhance the look of your workbook by selecting a different effect scheme. The effect scheme applies to charts and graphic objects, and each scheme defines a border style, fill style, and added effect such as a drop shadow or glow. Excel offers more than 20 effect schemes.

To get the most out of Excel's effect schemes, you must apply a style to your chart, as described in Chapter 12.

Choose Workbook Effects

1 Open or switch to the workbook you want to format.

2 Click the **Page Layout** tab.

3 Click **Effects** (⬚).

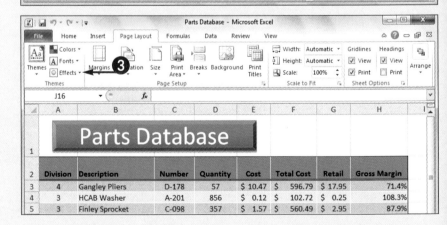

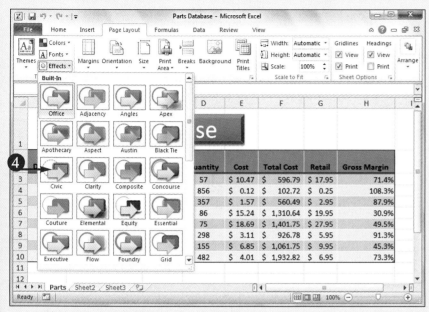

④ Click the effect scheme you want to apply.

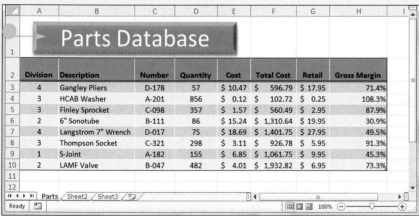

● Excel applies the effect scheme to the workbook's charts and graphics.

Can I create a custom effect scheme?
No. Unlike with the color schemes and font schemes described earlier in this chapter, Excel does not have a feature that enables you to create your own effect scheme.

Why are all the effect schemes the same color?
The color you see in the effect schemes depends on the color scheme you have applied to your workbook. If you apply a different color scheme, as described in "Modify the Workbook Colors," you will see a different color in the effect schemes. If you want to use a custom effect color, create a custom color scheme and change the Accent 1 color to the color you want.

Apply a Workbook Theme

You can give your workbook a completely new look by selecting a different workbook theme. Each theme consists of the workbook's colors, fonts, and effects. Excel offers more than 20 predefined workbook themes.

To get the most out of Excel's workbook themes, you must apply styles to your ranges, as described in Chapter 5; and to your charts, as described in Chapter 12.

Apply a Workbook Theme

① Open or switch to the workbook you want to format.

② Click the **Page Layout** tab.

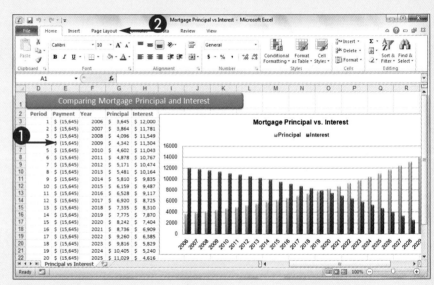

③ Click **Themes** (▣).

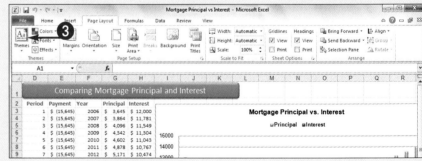

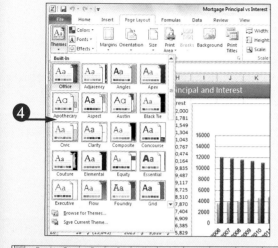

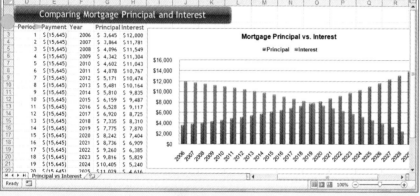

④ Click the workbook theme you want to apply.

● Excel applies the theme to the workbook.

Can I create my own workbook theme?
Yes, by following these steps:

① Format the workbook with a color scheme, font scheme, and effect scheme, as described in the previous three sections.

② Click the **Page Layout** tab.

③ Click 🗛.

④ Click **Save Current Theme**.

The Save Current Theme dialog box appears.

⑤ Type a name for the custom theme.

⑥ Click **Save**.

Chapter 10

Analyzing Excel Data

You can get more out of Excel by performing *data analysis*, which is the application of tools and techniques to organize, study, and reach conclusions about a specific collection of information.

In this chapter you learn how to sort and filter a range, apply data validation rules to a range, convert a range to a table, create a data table, and summarize data using subtotals.

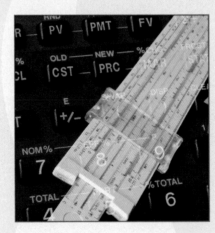

Sort a Range

You can make a range easier to read and easier to analyze by sorting the data based on the values in one or more columns.

You can sort the data in either ascending or descending order. An ascending sort arranges the values alphabetically from A to Z, or numerically from 0 to 9; a descending sort arranges the values alphabetically from Z to A, or numerically from 9 to 0.

Sort a Range

① Click any cell in the range you want to sort.

② Click the **Data** tab.

③ Click **Sort** (⊞).

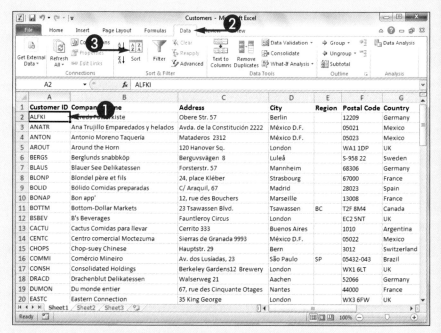

The Sort dialog box appears.

④ Click the **Sort by** ⊡ and then click the field you want to use for the main sort level.

⑤ Click the **Order** ⊡ and then click a sort order for the field.

⑥ To sort on another field, click **Add Level**.

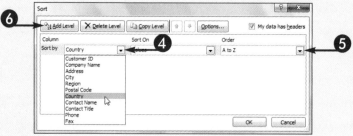

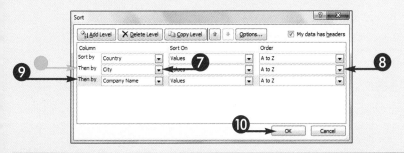

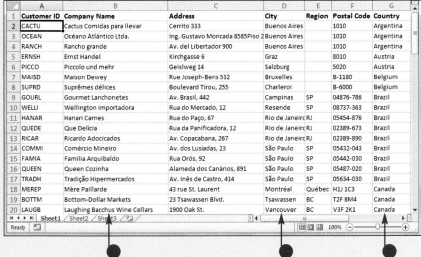

Excel adds another sort level.

7 Click the **Then by** ⊡ and then click the field you want to use for the sort level.

8 Click the **Order** ⊡ and then click a sort order for the field.

9 Repeat Steps **6** to **8** to add more sort levels as needed.

10 Click **OK**.

Excel sorts the range.

Is there a faster way to sort a range?
Yes, as long as you only need to sort your range on a single column. First, click in any cell inside the column you want to use for the sort. Click the **Data** tab and then click one of the following buttons in the Sort & Filter group:

⬆	Click for an ascending sort.
⬇	Click for a descending sort.

How do I sort a range using the values in a row instead of a column?
Excel normally sorts a range from top to bottom based on the values in one or more columns. However, you can tell Excel to sort the range from left to right based on the values in one or more rows. Follow Steps **1** to **3** to display the Sort dialog box. Click **Options** to display the Sort Options dialog box, select the **Sort left to right** option (○ changes to ◉), and then click **OK**.

Filter a Range

You can analyze table data much faster by filtering the data. *Filtering* a table means that you configure a field so that you only view the table records that you want to work with. One way to do this is to use the AutoFilter feature, which presents you with a list of check boxes for each unique value in a field. You filter the data by activating the check boxes for the records you want to see.

Filter a Range

1 Click inside the table.

2 Click the **Data** tab.

3 Click **Filter** (⛁).

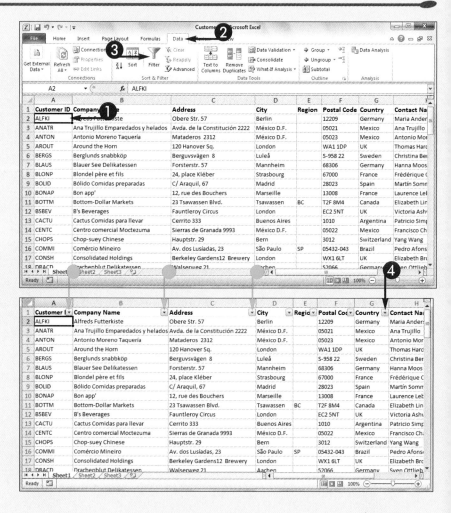

● Excel adds ⏷ to each field.

4 Click ⏷ for the field you want to use as the filter.

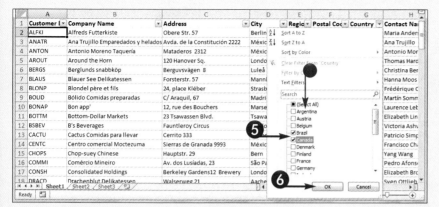

● Excel displays a list of the unique values in the field.

❺ Click the check box for each value you want to see (☐ changes to ☑).

❻ Click **OK**.

● Excel filters the table to show only those records that have the field values you selected.

● Excel displays the number of records found.

● The field's drop-down list displays a filter icon (🔽).

❼ To remove the filter, click **Clear** (🔽).

Simplify It

Can I create more sophisticated filters?
Yes, by following these steps:

❶ Follow Steps **1** to **4**.

❷ Click **Number Filters**.

Note: If the field is a date field, click Date Filters; if the field is a text field, click Text Filters.

❸ Click the filter you want to use.

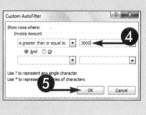

❹ Type the value you want to use, or use the list box to select a unique value from the field.

❺ Click **OK**.

Set Data Validation Rules

You can make Excel data entry more efficient by setting up data entry cells to accept only certain values. To do this, you can set up a cell with data validation criteria that specify the allowed value or values.

Excel also lets you tell the user what to enter by defining an input message that appears when the user selects the cell.

Set Data Validation Rules

① Click the cell you want to restrict.

② Click the **Data** tab.

③ Click **Data Validation** (▦).

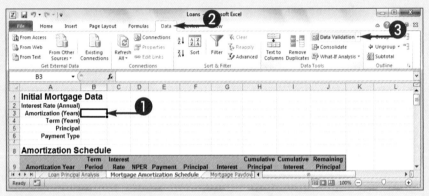

The Data Validation dialog box appears.

④ Click the **Settings** tab.

⑤ In the Allow list, click the type of data you want to allow in the cell.

⑥ Use the Data list to click the operator you want to use to define the allowable data.

⑦ Specify the validation criteria, such as the Maximum and Minimum allowable values shown here.

Note: *The criteria boxes you see depend on the operator you chose in Step 6.*

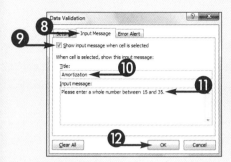

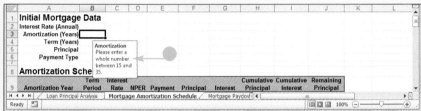

8 Click the **Input Message** tab.

9 Make sure the **Show input message when cell is selected** check box is clicked (☑).

10 Type a message title in the Title text box.

11 Type the message you want to display in the Input message text box.

12 Click **OK**.

Excel configures the cell to accept only values that meet your criteria.

● When the user selects the cell, the input message appears.

Simplify It

Can I configure the cell to display a message if the user tries to enter an invalid value?
Yes. Follow Steps **1** to **3** to open the Data Validation dialog box, and then click the **Error Alert** tab. Make sure the **Show error alert after invalid data is entered** check box is clicked (☑), and then specify the Style, Title, and Error Message. Click **OK**.

How do I remove data validation from a cell?
If you no longer need to use data validation on a cell, you should clear the settings. Follow Steps **1** to **3** to display the Data Validation dialog box and then click **Clear All**. Excel removes all the validation criteria, as well as the input message and the error alert. Click **OK**.

Convert a Range to a Table

You can apply Excel's powerful table tools to any range by first converting that range to a table. In Excel, a *table* is a collection of related information with an organizational structure that makes it easy to add, edit, and sort data.

A table is a type of database where the data is organized into rows and columns: Each column represents a database field, and each row represents a database record.

Convert a Range to a Table

1 Click a cell within the range that you want to convert to a table.

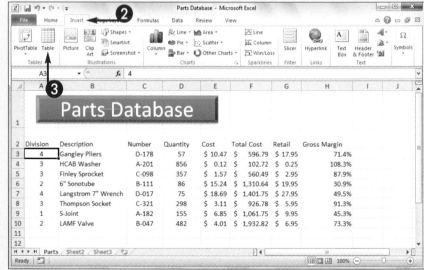

2 Click the **Insert** tab.

3 Click **Table** (⊞).

Note: You can also choose the Table command by pressing Ctrl + T.

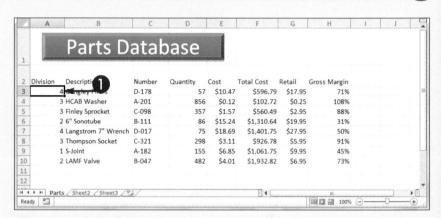

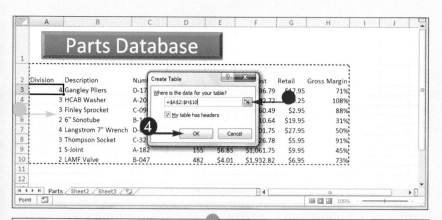

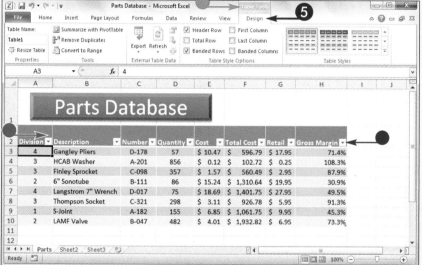

The Create Table dialog box appears.

● Excel selects the range that it will convert to a table.

● If you want to change the range, click 📧, drag the mouse ⇩ over the new range, and then click 📧.

④ Click **OK**.

Excel converts the range to a table.

● Excel applies a table format to the range.

● The Table Tools contextual tab appears.

● AutoFilter drop-down lists appear in each field heading.

⑤ Click the **Design** tab to see Excel's table design tools.

Simplify It

How do I add records to the table?
To add a record to the end of the table, click inside the table, press `Ctrl` + `↓` and then `Ctrl` + `→` to move to the last field in the last record, and then press `Tab`. To add a record within the table, right-click the record above where you want to insert the new record, click **Insert**, and then click **Table Rows Above**.

How do I convert a table back into a range?
If you no longer require the table tools, you can convert the table back into a regular range. Select any cell within the table, click the **Design** tab, and then click **Convert to Range** (📧). When Excel asks you to confirm, click **Yes**. Excel removes the AutoFilter drop-down lists and hides the Table Tools contextual tab.

Create a Data Table

If you are interested in studying the effect a range of values has on the formula, you can set up a *data table*. This is a table that consists of the formula you are using, and multiple input values for that formula. Excel automatically creates a solution to the formula for each different input value.

Do not confuse data tables with the Excel tables that you learned about in "Convert a Range to a Table." A data table is a special range that Excel uses to calculate multiple solutions to a formula.

Create a Data Table

1 Type the input values:

To enter the values in a column, start the column one cell down and one cell to the left of the cell containing the formula, as shown here.

To enter the values in a row, start the row one cell up and one cell to the right of the cell containing the formula.

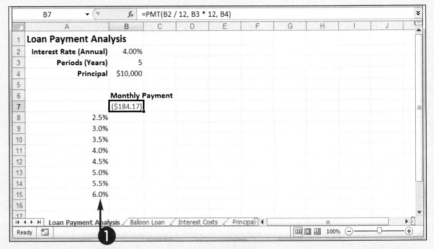

2 Select the range that includes the input values and the formula.

3 Click the **Data** tab.

4 Click **What-If Analysis** (⬛).

5 Click **Data Table**.

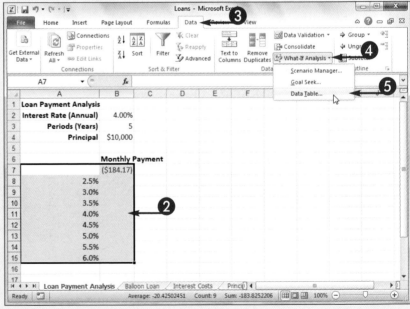

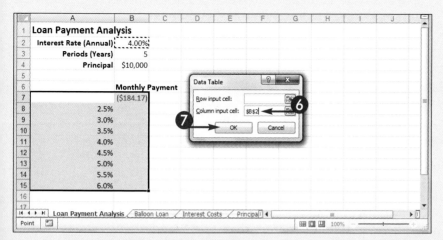

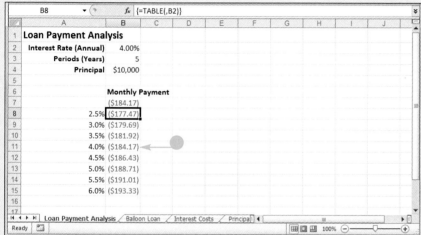

The Data Table dialog box appears.

⑥ Specify the formula cell you want to use as the data table's input cell:

If the input values are in a column, enter the input cell's address in the Column input cell text box.

If you entered the input values in a row, enter the input cell's address in the Row input cell text box.

⑦ Click **OK**.

● Excel displays the results.

What is what-if analysis?
The technique called *what-if analysis* is perhaps the most basic method for analyzing worksheet data. With what-if analysis, you first calculate a formula D, based on the input from variables A, B, and C. You then say, "What happens to the result if I change the value of variable A?", "What happens if I change B or C?", and so on.

When I try to delete part of the data table, I get an error. Why?
The data table results are created as an *array formula*, which is a special formula that Excel treats as a unit. This means that you cannot move or delete part of the results. If you need to work with the data table results, you must first select the entire results range.

Summarize Data with Subtotals

When you need to summarize your data, Excel offers a feature that enables you to quickly and easily add subtotals to a range of data.

Although you can use formulas and worksheet functions to summarize your data in various ways, including sums, averages, counts,

maximums, and minimums, if you are in a hurry, or if you just need a quick summary of your data, you can get Excel to do most of the work for you. The secret here is a feature called *automatic subtotals*, which are formulas that Excel adds to a worksheet automatically.

Summarize Data with Subtotals

1 Click a cell within the range you want to subtotal.

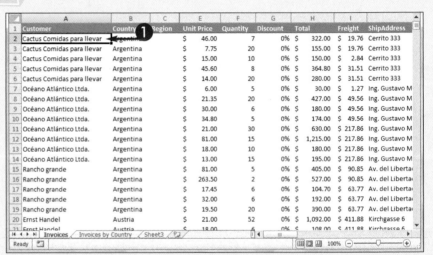

2 Click the **Data** tab.

3 Click **Subtotal** (📇).

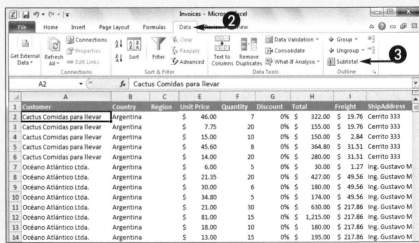

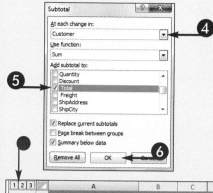

The Subtotal dialog box appears.

④ Click the **At each change in** ⊡ and then click the column you want to use to group the subtotals.

⑤ In the Add subtotal to list, click the check box for the column you want to summarize (☐ changes to ☑).

⑥ Click **OK**.

● Excel calculates the subtotals and adds them into the range.

● Excel adds outline symbols to the range.

Do I need to prepare my worksheet to use subtotals?
Excel sets up automatic subtotals based on data groupings in a selected field. For example, if you ask for subtotals based on the Customer field, Excel runs down the Customer column and creates a new subtotal each time the name changes. To get useful summaries, then, you need to sort the range on the field containing the data groupings you are interested in.

Can I only calculate totals?
No. The word "subtotal" here is a bit misleading because you can summarize more than just totals. You can also count values, calculate the average of the values, determine the maximum or minimum value, and more. To change the summary calculation, follow Steps **1** to **4**, click the **Use function** ⊡, and then click the function you want to use for the summary.

Chapter 11

Visualizing Data with Excel Charts

You can take a worksheet full of numbers and display them as a chart. Visualizing your data in this way makes the data easier to understand and analyze. To help you see your data exactly the way you want, Excel offers a wide variety of chart types, including pie charts, column charts, and stock charts. Excel also offers a large number of chart options that enable you to add chart titles and data labels, control the chart legend and gridlines, format the chart layout and style, change the chart type, and more.

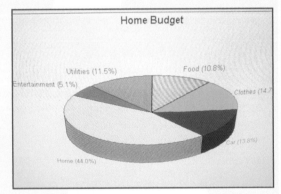

Examining Chart Elements

A *chart* is a graphic representation of spreadsheet data that uses columns, points, pie wedges, and other forms to represent numbers from a select range. As the data in the spreadsheet changes, the chart also changes to reflect the new numbers. To get the most out of charts, you need to familiarize yourself with the basic chart elements.

Category Axis
The axis (usually the X axis) that contains the category groupings.

Chart Title
The title of the chart.

Data Marker
A symbol that represents a specific data value. The symbol used depends on the chart type.

Data Series
A collection of related data values. Normally, the marker for each value in a series has the same pattern.

Data Value
A single piece of data. Also called a *data point*.

Gridlines
Optional horizontal and vertical extensions of the axis tick marks. These make data values easier to read.

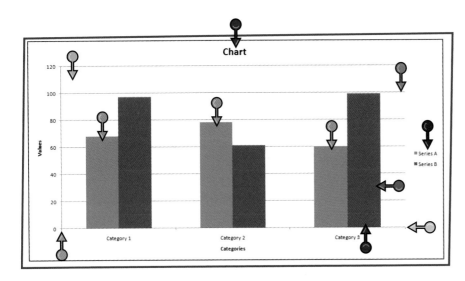

Plot Area
The area bounded by the category and value axes. It contains the data points and gridlines.

Value Axis
The axis (usually the Y axis) that contains the data values.

Legend
A guide that shows the colors, patterns, and symbols used by the markers for each data series.

Understanding Chart Types

Excel offers 11 different types of charts, including column charts, bar charts, line charts, and pie charts. The chart type you use depends on the type of data and how you want to present that data visually. Although you must select a particular chart type when you first construct your chart, you can quickly and easily change to a different chart type later on if you need to.

Chart Type	Description
Area	A chart that shows the relative contributions over time that each data series makes to the whole picture.
Bar	A chart that compares distinct items or shows single items at distinct intervals. A bar chart is laid out with categories along the vertical axis and values along the horizontal axis.
Bubble	A chart that is similar to an XY chart, except that there are three data series, and in the third series the individual plot points are displayed as bubbles (the larger the value, the larger the bubble).
Column	A chart that, like a bar chart, compares distinct items or shows single items at distinct intervals. However, a column chart is laid out with categories along the horizontal axis and values along the vertical axis.
Doughnut	A chart that, like a pie chart, shows the proportion of the whole that is contributed by each value in a data series. The advantage of a doughnut chart is that you can plot multiple data series.
Line	A chart that shows how a data series changes over time. The category (X) axis usually represents a progression of even increments (such as days or months), and the series points are plotted on the value (Y) axis.
Pie	A chart that shows the proportion of the whole that is contributed by each value in a single data series. The whole is represented as a circle (the "pie"), and each value is displayed as a proportional "slice" of the circle.
Radar	A chart that makes comparisons within a data series and between data series relative to a center point. Each category is shown with a value axis extending from the center point.
Stock	A chart that is designed to plot stock market prices, such as a stock's daily high, low, and closing values.
Surface	A chart that analyzes two sets of data and determines the optimum combination of the two.
XY	A chart that shows the relationship between numeric values in two different data series. It can also plot a series of data pairs in XY coordinates. (Also called a *scatter* chart.)

Create a Chart

You can create a chart from your Excel worksheet data with just a few mouse clicks. As shown in "Understanding Chart Types," Excel comes with 11 main chart types. However, each of these types has several predefined varieties, so in all Excel offers more than 70 default chart configurations, which means there should always be a type that best visualizes your data.

Regardless of the chart type you choose originally, you can change to a different chart type at any time. See "Select a Different Chart Type" later in this chapter.

Create a Chart

❶ Select the data that you want to visualize in a chart.

● If your data includes headings, be sure to include those headings in the selection.

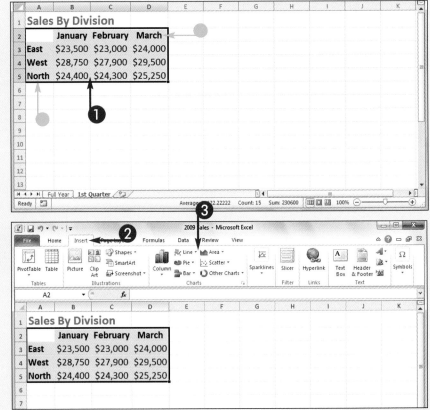

❷ Click the **Insert** tab.

❸ Click a chart type.

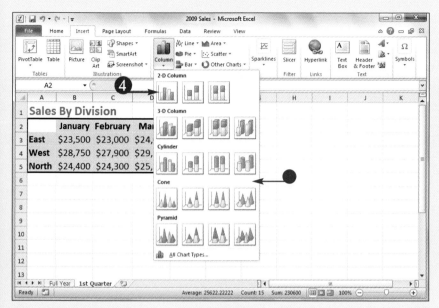

● Excel displays a gallery of configurations for the chart type.

④ Click the chart configuration you want to use.

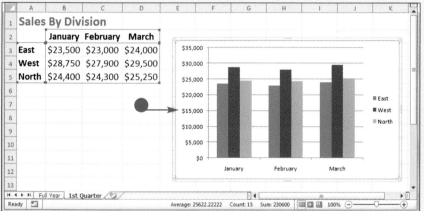

● Excel inserts the chart.

The tasks in the rest of this chapter show you how to configure, format, and move the chart.

Simplify It

Is there a way to create a chart on a separate sheet?
Yes. You can use a special workbook sheet called a *chart sheet*. If you have not yet created your chart, select the worksheet data, right-click any worksheet tab, and then click **Insert** to display the Insert dialog box. Click the **General** tab, click **Chart**, and then click **OK**. Excel creates a new chart sheet and inserts the chart.

Add Chart Titles

You can make your chart easier to read and easier to understand by adding one or more titles to the chart. For example, you can add a *chart title*, which is a title that appears at the top of the chart and is usually a word or short phrase that describes the chart data.

You can also add titles to the chart axes. The *primary horizontal axis title* is a title that appears below the chart's category (X) axis; the *primary vertical axis title* is a title that appears the left of the chart's value (Y) axis.

① Click the chart.

② Click the **Layout** tab.

③ Click **Chart Title** (▣).

④ Click **Above Chart**.

● Excel adds the title.

⑤ Type the title.

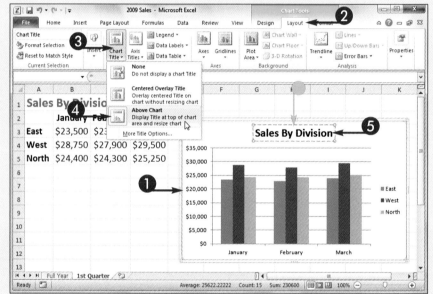

⑥ Click **Axis Titles** (▣).

⑦ Click **Primary Horizontal Axis Title**.

⑧ Click **Title Below Axis**.

● Excel adds the title.

⑨ Type the title.

⑩ Click ▣.

⑪ Click **Primary Vertical Axis Title**.

⑫ Click **Rotated Title** (not shown).

● Excel adds the title.

⑬ Type the title.

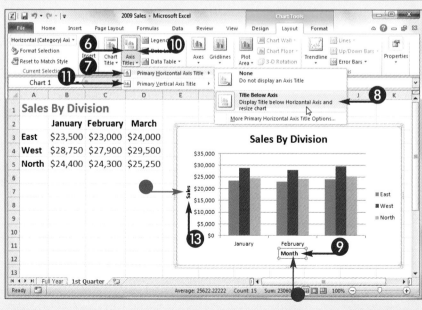

Add Data Labels

You can make your chart easier to read by adding data labels. A *data label* is a small text box that appears in or near a data marker and displays the value of that data point.

Excel offers several position options for the data labels, and these options depend on the

chart type. For example, with a column chart you can place the data labels within or above each column, and for a line chart you can place the labels to the left or right, or above or below, the data marker.

Add Data Labels

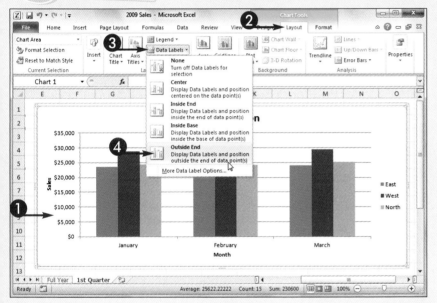

① Click the chart.

② Click the **Layout** tab.

③ Click **Data Labels** (📊).

④ Click the position you want to use for the data labels.

Note: *Remember that the position options you see depend on the chart type.*

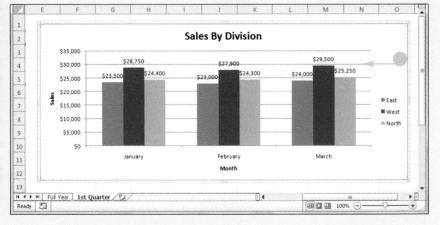

● Excel adds the labels to the chart.

Position the Chart Legend

You can change the position of the chart *legend*, which is a box that appears alongside the chart and serves to identify the colors associated with each data series in the chart. By default, the legend appears to the right of the chart's plot area, but you might prefer a different location.

For example, you might find the legend easier to read if it appears to the left of the chart. Alternatively, if you want more horizontal room to display your chart, you can move the legend above or below the chart.

Position the Chart Legend

① Click the chart.

② Click the **Layout** tab.

③ Click **Legend** (▣).

④ Click the position you want to use for the legend.

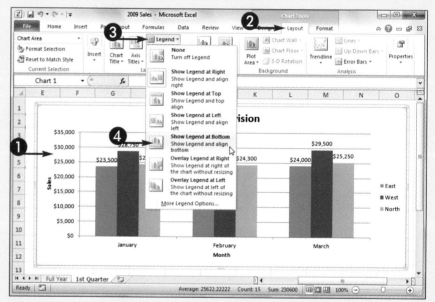

● Excel moves the legend.

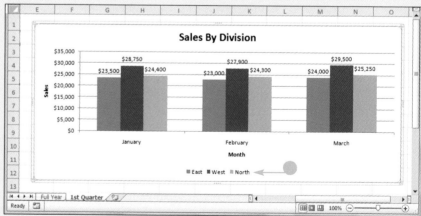

Display Chart Gridlines

You can make your chart easier to read and easier to analyze by adding gridlines. Horizontal gridlines extend from the vertical (value) axis and are useful with area, bubble, and column charts. Vertical gridlines extend from the horizontal (category) axis and are useful with bar and line charts.

Major gridlines are gridlines associated with the *major units*: the values you see displayed on the vertical and horizontal axes; *minor gridlines* are gridlines associated with the *minor units*: values between each major unit.

Display Chart Gridlines

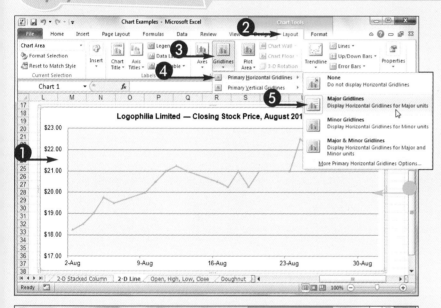

1. Click the chart.
2. Click the **Layout** tab.
3. Click **Gridlines** (⊞).
4. Click **Primary Horizontal Gridlines**.
5. Click the horizontal gridline option you prefer.

● Excel displays the horizontal gridlines.

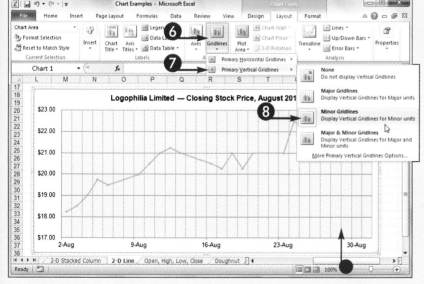

6. Click ⊞.
7. Click **Primary Vertical Gridlines**.
8. Click the vertical gridline option you prefer.

● Excel displays the vertical gridlines.

Display a Data Table

You can make it easier for yourself and others to interpret your chart by adding a data table. A *data table* is a tabular grid where each row is a data series from the chart, each column is a chart category, and each cell is a chart data point.

Excel gives you the option of displaying the data table with or without *legend keys*, which are markers that identify each series.

① Click the chart.

② Click the **Layout** tab.

③ Click **Data Table** (▦).

④ Click **Show Data Table with Legend Keys**.

● If you prefer not to display the legend keys, click **Show Data Table**.

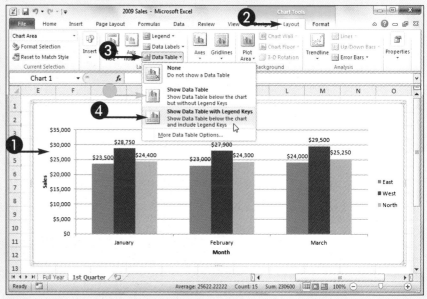

● Excel adds the data table below the chart.

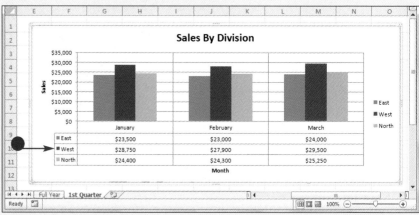

Change the Chart Layout and Style

You can quickly format your chart by applying a different chart layout and a different chart style. The chart layout includes elements such as the titles, data labels, legend, gridlines, and data table. Excel's Quick Layouts feature enables you to apply these elements in different combinations with just a few mouse clicks.

The chart style represents the colors used by the chart data markers and background.

Change the Chart Layout and Style

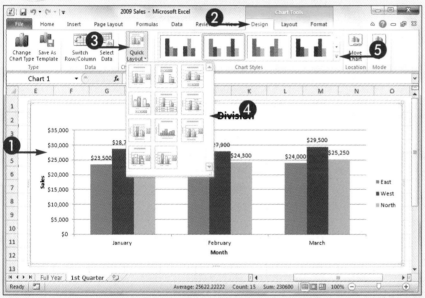

① Click the chart.

② Click the **Design** tab.

③ Click **Quick Layout** (📊).

④ Click the layout you want to use.

Excel applies the layout.

⑤ Click the **Chart Styles** ⏷.

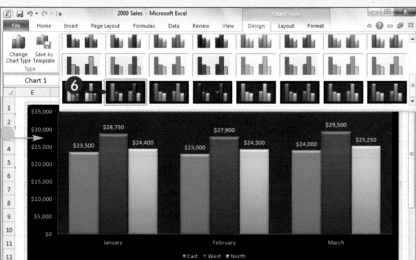

⑥ Click the chart style you want to use.

● Excel applies the style to the chart.

Select a Different Chart Type

If you feel that the current chart type is not showing your data in the best way, you can change the chart type with just a few mouse clicks. For example, you might want to change a bar chart to a pie chart or a line chart to a stock chart.

As you will see in the Tips on the following page, you can also save yourself some work by configuring Excel with a new default chart type, and by saving the current chart type and chart formatting as a template that you can reuse later on.

Select a Different Chart Type

1 Click the chart.

2 Click the **Design** tab.

3 Click **Change Chart Type** (📊).

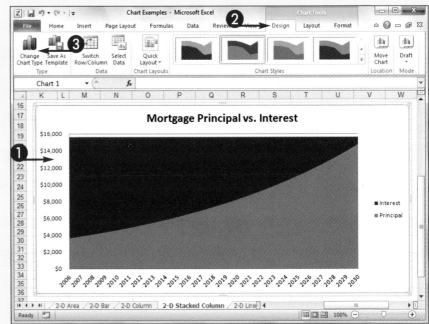

The Change Chart Type dialog box appears.

4 Click the chart type you want to use.

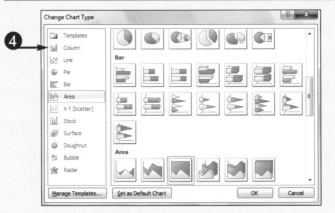

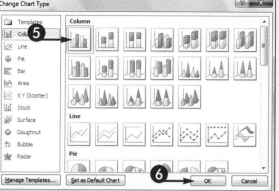

Excel displays the chart type configurations.

5 Click the configuration you want to use.

6 Click **OK**.

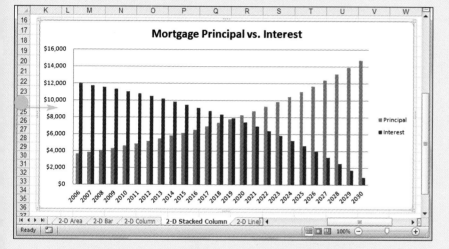

Excel applies the new chart type.

Can I tell Excel to always use a particular chart type each time I create a new chart?
Yes, you can configure that chart type as the default type for new charts. Follow Steps **1** to **5** to open the Change Chart Type dialog box and select a chart type and configuration. Click the **Set as Default Chart** button, and then click **OK**.

Can I save the chart type and formatting so that I can reuse it later on a different chart?
Yes. You do this by saving your work as a chart template. Follow the steps in this section and in the previous few sections of this chapter to set the chart type, titles, labels, legend position, gridlines, layout, and style. Click the **Design** tab, click **Save as Template** (🖼), type a name for the template, and then click **Save**. To reuse the template, follow Steps **1** to **3**, click **Templates**, click your template, and then click **OK**.

Chapter 12

Formatting Excel Charts

You use Excel charts to visualize worksheet data, and you can make these visualizations more eye-catching and more effective by formatting chart elements.

In this chapter, you first learn the general technique for formatting any chart elements. In the rest of the chapter, you learn specific chart customization techniques, including formatting the chart background, customizing a chart element's outline, applying special effects to a chart element, and applying a style to a chart element.

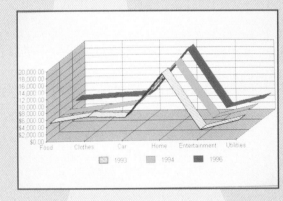

Format Chart Elements

You can customize the look of your chart by formatting the various chart elements. These elements include the axes, titles, labels, legend, gridlines, data series, plot area (the area where the chart data appears), and the chart area (the overall background of the chart).

You can format chart elements using either the Format dialog box or the Ribbon. The rest of the sections in this chapter provide you with more detail on using the Ribbon commands.

Format Chart Elements

Format Chart Elements Using the Format Dialog Box

① Click the chart element you want to format.

② Click the **Format** tab.

● You can also select a chart element by clicking the **Chart Title** ⏷ and then clicking the object.

③ Click **Format Selection** (🖑).

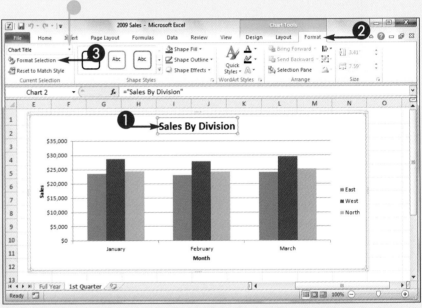

The Format dialog box appears for the object you selected. Here, it is the Format Chart Title dialog box.

④ Click a tab.

⑤ Change the formatting options.

⑥ Repeat Steps **4** and **5** to set other formatting options.

⑦ Click **Close**.

Excel applies the formatting.

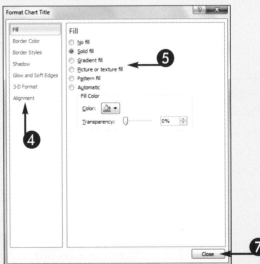

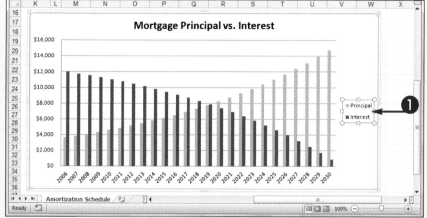

Format Chart Elements Using the Ribbon

1️⃣ Click the chart element you want to format.

2️⃣ Click the **Format** tab.

3️⃣ Use the Ribbon controls to change the formatting options.

Note: Not all of the Ribbon controls will be available for each chart element.

Excel applies the formatting.

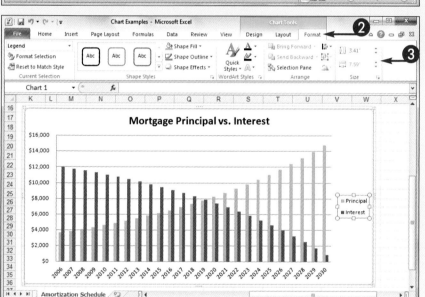

Are there any formatting shortcuts I can use?
Yes. Excel offers several methods you can use to quickly open the Format dialog box. If you are using your mouse, position ⌕ over the element you want to format, and then double-click. From the keyboard, first click the chart element you want to format and then press **Ctrl** + **1**. You can also right-click the chart element and then click **Format** *Element* (where *Element* is the name of the element).

How do I know where to click to select a chart element?
The easiest way to be sure you are clicking the correct element is to position ⌕ over the object. If ⌕ is positioned correctly, a banner appears and the banner text displays the name of the chart element. If the banner does not appear, or if the banner displays a chart element name other than the one you want to format, move ⌕ until the correct banner appears.

Customize a Chart Element Background

You can add visual interest to a chart element by customizing the element's background, or what Excel calls the *fill*.

Most fills consist of a single color, but you can also apply a color gradient, a texture, or even a picture. However, you should be careful about

the background you choose for certain chart elements. Since some chart elements — particularly the chart area, plot area, value axis, and category axis — display data, be sure to choose a background that does not make that data difficult to read.

Customize a Chart Element Background

Apply a Color Fill

1 Click the chart element you want to format.

2 Click the **Format** tab.

3 Click the **Shape Fill** ⏷.

4 Click the color you want to apply.

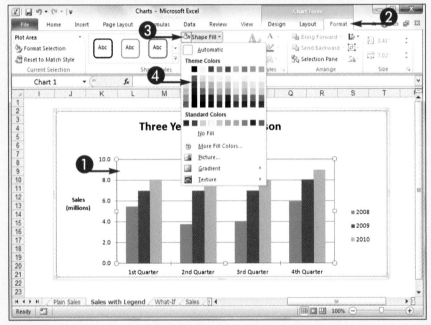

● Excel formats the element's background with the color you selected.

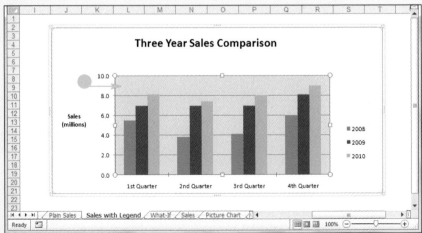

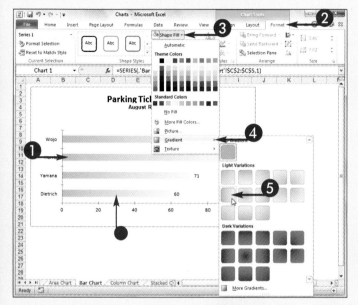

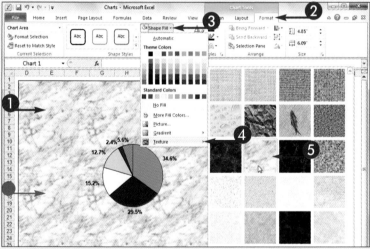

Apply a Gradient Fill

1️⃣ Click the chart element you want to format.

2️⃣ Click the **Format** tab.

3️⃣ Click the **Shape Fill** ⊡.

4️⃣ Click **Gradient**.

5️⃣ Click the gradient you want to apply.

⬤ Excel formats the element's background with the gradient you selected.

Apply a Texture Fill

1️⃣ Click the chart element you want to format.

2️⃣ Click the **Format** tab.

3️⃣ Click the **Shape Fill** ⊡.

4️⃣ Click **Texture**.

5️⃣ Click the texture you want to apply.

⬤ Excel formats the element's background with the texture you selected.

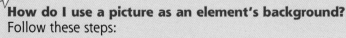

How do I use a picture as an element's background?
Follow these steps:

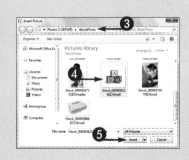

1️⃣ Follow Steps **1** to **3**.

2️⃣ Click **Picture**.

3️⃣ Click the folder that contains the image file.

4️⃣ Click the image file you want to use as the background.

5️⃣ Click **Insert**.

Set a Chart Element's Outline

You can make a chart element stand out by customizing the element's outline, which refers to the border that appears around the element, as well as to single-line elements, such as gridlines and axes.

You can customize the outline's color, its weight — that is, its thickness — and whether the line is solid or consists of a series of dots or dashes.

Set a Chart Element's Outline

① Click the chart element you want to format.

② Click the **Format** tab.

③ Click the **Shape Outline** ⊡.

④ Click the color you want to apply.

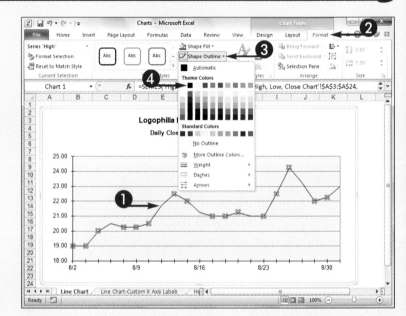

⑤ Click the **Shape Outline** ⊡.

⑥ Click **Weight**.

⑦ Click the line thickness you want to apply.

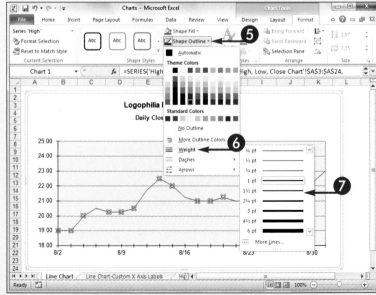

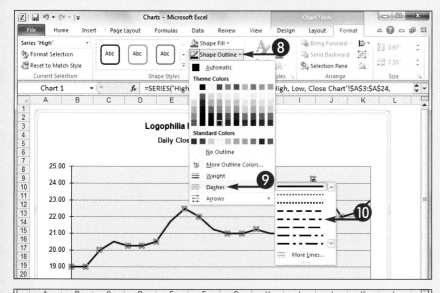

8 Click the **Shape Outline** □.

9 Click **Dashes**.

10 Click the line style you want to apply.

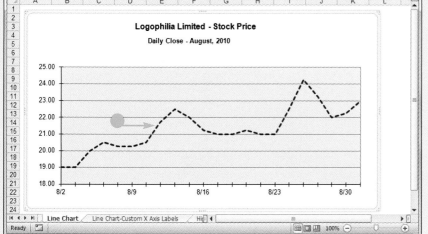

● Excel formats the element's outline with the color, weight, and style you selected.

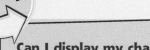

Can I display my chart with a rounded outline?
Yes. Follow these steps:

1 Click the chart border to select the chart area element.

2 Click the **Format** tab.

3 Click **Format Selection** (🖫).

4 Click the **Border Styles** tab.

5 Click **Rounded corners** (☐ changes to ☑).

6 Click **Close**.

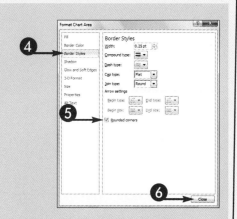

Add Effects to a Chart Element

You can make your chart elements more visually striking by customizing them with special effects.

For most chart elements, you can add one or more effects, including a shadow, glow, soft edges, or bevel. In all cases, however, make sure that the effects you apply do not make the element more difficult to read or to decipher, and that the effects you use do not distract the reader from the chart itself.

Add Effects to a Chart Element

Add a Shadow Effect

1. Click the chart element you want to format.

2. Click the **Format** tab.

3. Click the **Shape Effects** ⊡.

4. Click **Shadow**.

5. Click the shadow effect you want to apply.

● Excel formats the element with the shadow you selected.

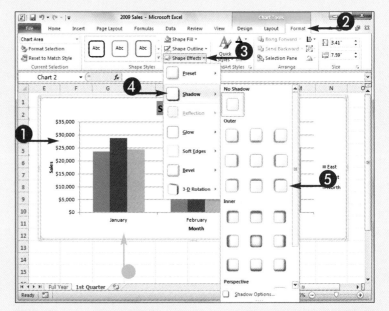

Add a Glow Effect

1. Click the chart element you want to format.

2. Click the **Format** tab.

3. Click the **Shape Effects** ⊡.

4. Click **Glow**.

5. Click the glow effect you want to apply.

● Excel formats the element with the glow you selected.

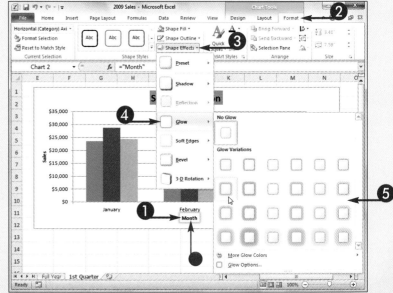

206

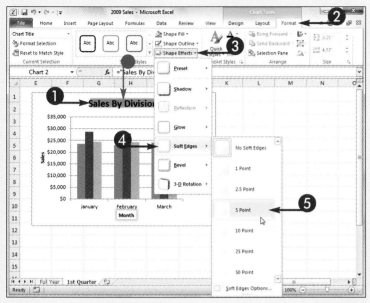

Add a Soft Edges Effect

1. Click the chart element you want to format.

2. Click the **Format** tab.

3. Click the **Shape Effects** ⏷.

4. Click **Soft Edges**.

5. Click the soft edges effect you want to apply.

● Excel formats the element with the soft edges you selected.

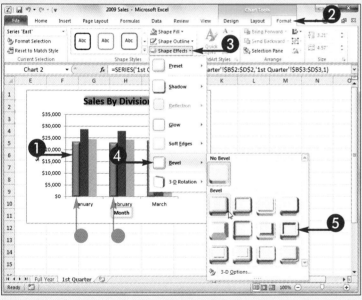

Add a Bevel Effect

1. Click the chart element you want to format.

2. Click the **Format** tab.

3. Click the **Shape Effects** ⏷.

4. Click **Bevel**.

5. Click the bevel effect you want to apply.

● Excel formats the element with the bevel you selected.

Simplify It

The shadow I selected is not very noticeable. How can I get a better shadow effect?
Excel offers several controls that enable you to manually adjust various aspects of the shadow.
Follow Steps **1** to **4** in "Add a Shadow Effect" and then click **Shadow Options**. Either use the
Size spin box to increase the size of the shadow, or use the Distance spin box to increase the
space between the chart element and the shadow. Click **Close** when you are done.

Apply a Style to a Chart Element

You can reduce the time it takes to format a chart element by applying a style to that element. Excel comes with more than 40 predefined element styles, each of which is a collection of chart formatting features.

Each style includes one or more of the following formatting features: a background,

which is usually either a solid color or a color gradient; an outline, which is usually a solid line with a color that matches or complements the background; and one or more special effects, such as a shadow or bevel.

Apply a Style to a Chart Element

❶ Click the chart element you want to format.

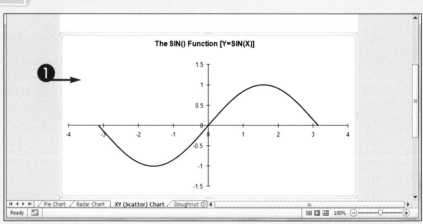

❷ Click the **Format** tab.

❸ Click the **Shape Styles** ⊡.

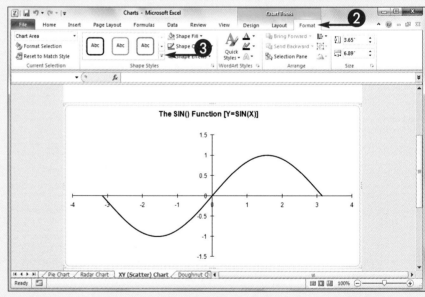

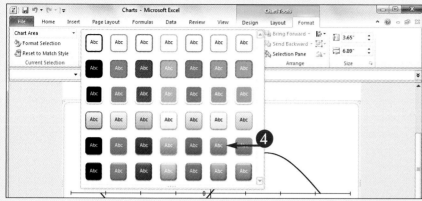

Excel displays the Shape Styles gallery.

④ Click the style you want to apply.

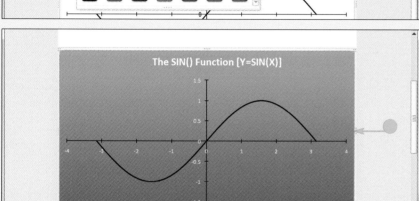

● Excel applies the style.

How do I remove a style from a chart element?
Unfortunately, Excel does not offer a simple method for removing a style. Instead, you must remove the background, outline, and effects individually. To begin, click the chart element you want to work with, and then click the **Format** tab.

For the background, click the **Shape Fill** ⬚ and then click **No Fill**. For the outline, click the **Shape Outline** ⬚ and then click **No Outline**. For the special effects, click the **Shape Effects** ⬚, click **Preset**, and then click **No Presets**.

Chapter 13

Collaborating with Other People

Although you will most often create and edit an Excel workbook on your own, you may have some workbooks that require input from other people. For those times when you need to collaborate with other people on a workbook, Excel has the tools to get the job done.

In this chapter, you learn many ways to collaborate on a workbook, including adding

comments to a cell, sharing a workbook, e-mailing a workbook, and even working on a spreadsheet online. You also learn ways to make collaboration safer by protecting any data you do not want changed, tracking whatever changes are made by others, and accepting or rejecting those changes.

Add a Comment to a Cell

If you have received a workbook from another person, you can provide feedback to that person by adding a comment to a cell in the workbook. A comment is often the best way to give feedback because it does not change anything on the worksheet itself.

Comments are attached to a particular cell, and Excel displays an indicator on any cell that has a comment. When you hover your mouse pointer over such a cell, Excel displays the comment in a balloon.

Add a Comment to a Cell

Add a Comment

① Click the cell you want to comment on.

② Click the **Review** tab.

③ Click **New Comment** (▢).

Note: You can also right-click the cell and then click **Insert Comment**.

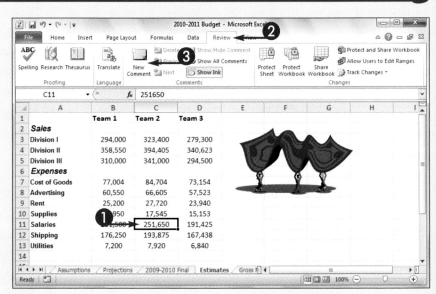

Excel displays a comment balloon.

● Excel precedes the comment with your Excel user name.

④ Type your comment.

⑤ Click outside the comment balloon.

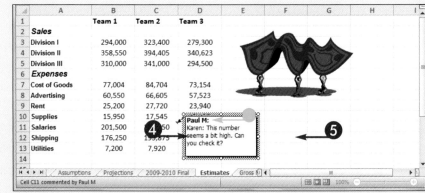

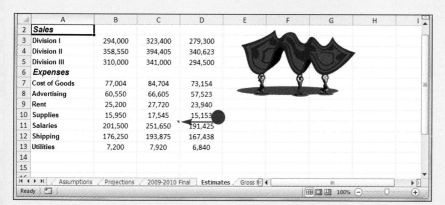

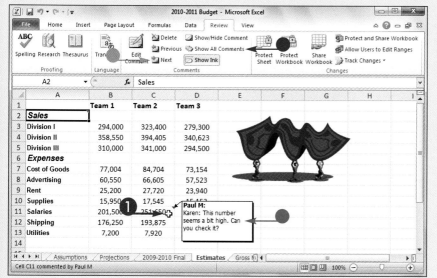

● Excel adds a comment indicator (⬜) to the top right corner of the cell.

View a Comment

1 Move the mouse ⇩ over the cell.

● Excel displays the comment in a balloon.

● In the **Review** tab, you can also click **Next** (▣) and **Previous** (▣) to run through the comments.

● In the **Review** tab, you can also click **Show All Comments** (▣) to display every comment at once.

Simplify It

Can I edit or remove a comment?
Yes. To edit an existing comment, click the cell that contains the comment, click the **Review** tab, click **Edit Comment** (▣) to open the comment in a balloon, and then edit the balloon text. To remove a comment, click the cell that contains the comment, click the **Review** tab, and then click **Delete** (▣).

How do I change my Excel user name?
When collaborating, your user name is important because it tells other people who added the comments. If your current user name consists of only your first name or your initials, you can change it. Click **File** and then click **Options** to open the Excel Options dialog box. Click the **General** tab and then use the User name text box to edit the name. Click **OK**. Note, however, that this does not change your user name in any existing comments.

Protect a Worksheet's Data

If you will be distributing a workbook to other people, you can enable Excel's options for safeguarding worksheet data by activating the sheet's protection feature. You can also configure the worksheet to require a password to unprotect it.

There are two main methods you can use to safeguard worksheet data: You can unlock only those cells that users are allowed to edit, and you can configure a range to require a password before it can be edited.

Protect a Worksheet's Data

1 Display the worksheet you want to protect.

2 Click the **Review** tab.

3 Click **Protect Sheet** (▦).

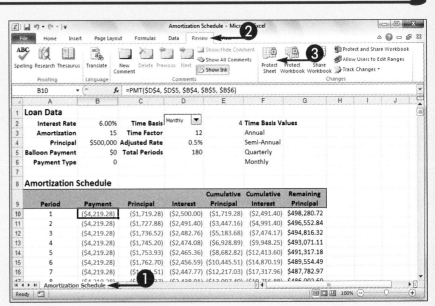

Excel displays the Protect Sheet dialog box.

4 Make sure the Protect worksheet and contents of locked cells check box is activated (☑).

5 Use the Password to unprotect sheet password box to type a password, if required.

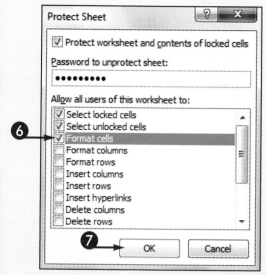

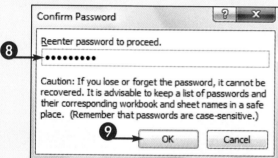

6 Click the check box beside each action that you want to allow unauthorized users to perform (☐ changes to ☑).

7 Click **OK**.

If you specified a password, Excel asks you to confirm the password.

8 Type the password.

9 Click **OK**.

If you want to make changes to a worksheet, click the **Review** tab, click **Unprotect Sheet** (📭), type the unprotect password, and then click **OK**.

Simplify It

When I protect a worksheet, no one can edit any of the cells. Is there a way to allow users to edit some of the cells?

Yes. This is useful if you have a data entry area or other range that you want other people to be able to edit, but you do not want them to alter any other part of the worksheet. First, unprotect the sheet if it is currently protected. Select the range you want to unlock, click **Home**, click **Format**, and then click **Lock Cell** to turn off that option for the selected range.

When I protect a worksheet, can I configure a range to require a password before a user can edit the range?

Yes. First, unprotect the sheet if it is currently protected. Select the range you want to protect, click the **Review** tab, and then click **Allow Users to Edit Ranges**. In the Allow Users to Edit Ranges dialog box, click **New** to open the New Range dialog box. Type a title for the range, use the Range password box to type a password, and then click **OK**. When Excel prompts you to reenter the password, type the password and then click **OK**.

Protect a Workbook's Structure and Windows

You can prevent unwanted changes to a workbook by activating protection for the workbook's windows and structure. You can also configure the workbook to require a password to unprotect it.

You should protect a workbook's structure when you do not want others to perform

actions such as adding or deleting worksheets; you should protect a workbook's windows when you do not want others to perform actions such as splitting a window or freezing panes. See the Tips on the following page to learn what Excel does when you protect a workbook's structure and windows.

Protect a Workbook's Structure and Windows

1 Display the workbook you want to protect.

2 Click the **Review** tab.

3 Click **Protect Workbook** (🗐).

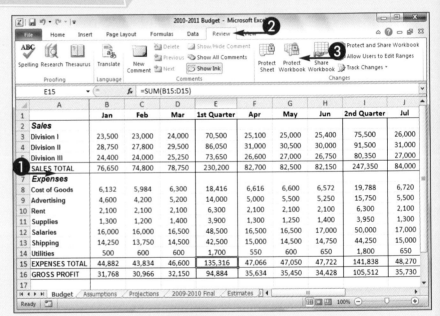

Excel displays the Protect Structure and Windows dialog box.

4 Click the **Structure** check box to protect the workbook's structure (☐ changes to ☑).

5 Click the **Windows** check box to protect the workbook's windows (☐ changes to ☑).

6 Type a password in the Password text box, if required.

7 Click **OK**.

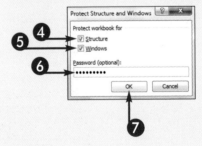

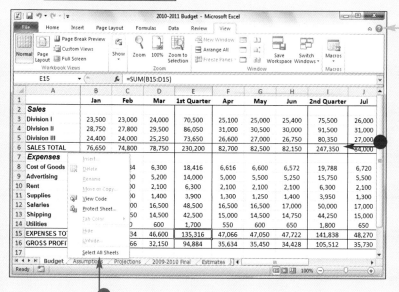

If you specified a password, Excel asks you to confirm it.

8 Type the password.

9 Click **OK**.

● If you protected the windows, Excel hides the window controls.

● If you protected the windows, Excel disables many window-related commands on the View tab.

● If you protected the structure, Excel disables most sheet-related commands on the sheet shortcut menu.

What happens when I protect a workbook's structure?
Excel disables most worksheet-related commands, including Insert Sheet, Delete Sheet, Rename Sheet, Move or Copy Sheet, Tab Color, Hide Sheet, and Unhide Sheet. Excel also prevents the Scenario Manager from creating a summary report.

What happens when I protect a workbook's windows?
Excel hides the window's Close, Maximize, and Minimize buttons. If the workbook is not maximized, Excel also disables the window borders, which means the window cannot be moved, sized, or closed. Excel also disables the View tab's New Window, Split, Freeze Panes, and View Side By Side commands when the window is active.

Share a Workbook with Other Users

You can allow multiple users to modify a workbook simultaneously by sharing the workbook. Once you have shared a workbook, other users can open the workbook via a network connection and edit the file at the same time.

When you share a workbook, Excel automatically begins tracking the changes made to the file. For more information on this feature, see "Track Workbook Changes" later in this chapter. Note, as well, that this task assumes you have saved the workbook in a folder that other people can access over the network.

Share a Workbook with Other Users

1 Display the workbook you want to share.

2 Click the **Review** tab.

3 Click **Share Workbook** (▦).

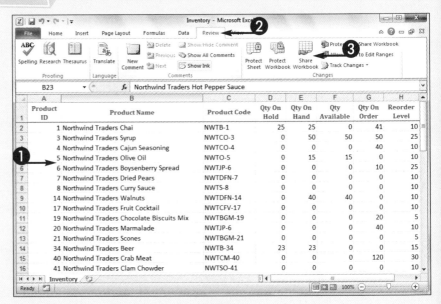

The Share Workbook dialog box appears.

4 Click the **Editing** tab.

5 Click the **Allow changes by more than one user at the same time** check box (☐ changes to ☑).

6 Click **OK**.

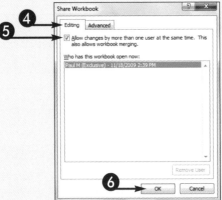

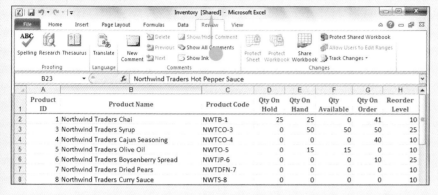

Excel tells you that it will now save the workbook.

7 Click **OK**.

Excel saves the workbook and activates sharing.

● Excel displays [Shared] in the title bar.

You and users on your network can now edit the workbook at the same time.

Simplify It

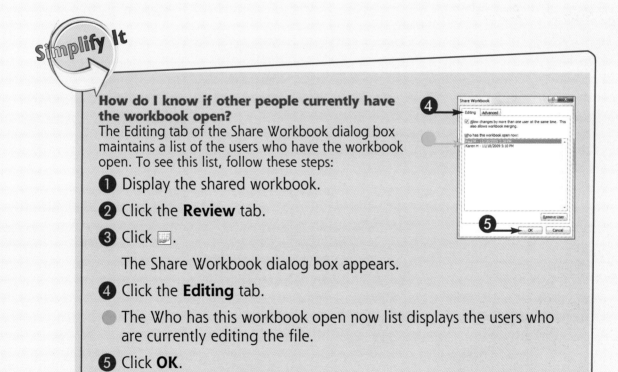

How do I know if other people currently have the workbook open?
The Editing tab of the Share Workbook dialog box maintains a list of the users who have the workbook open. To see this list, follow these steps:

1 Display the shared workbook.

2 Click the **Review** tab.

3 Click 🗔.

The Share Workbook dialog box appears.

4 Click the **Editing** tab.

● The Who has this workbook open now list displays the users who are currently editing the file.

5 Click **OK**.

Track Workbook Changes

If you want other people to make changes to a workbook, you can keep track of those changes so you can either accept or reject them (see "Accept or Reject Workbook Changes"). Excel's Track Changes feature enables you to do this.

When you turn on Track Changes, Excel monitors the activity of each reviewer and stores that reviewer's cell edits, row and column additions and deletions, range moves, worksheet insertions, and worksheet renames. When you open the workbook later on, you see all of these changes onscreen, along with the name of each person who made the change.

Track Workbook Changes

1 Display the workbook you want to track.

2 Click the **Review** tab.

3 Click **Track Changes** ().

4 Click **Highlight Changes**.

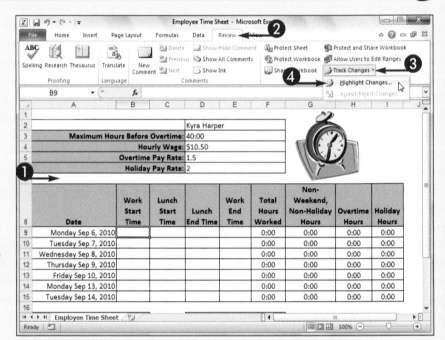

The Highlight Changes dialog box appears.

5 Click the **Track changes while editing** check box (changes to).

● Leave the When check box activated ( ) and leave All selected in the list.

● To learn more about the Who and Where options, see the Tips on the next page.

● Leave the Highlight changes on screen check box activated ( ) to view the workbook changes.

6 Click **OK**.

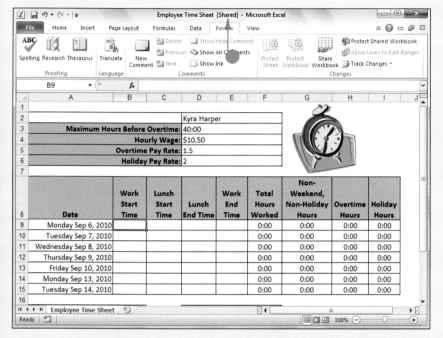

Excel tells you it will now save the workbook.

7 Click **OK**.

Excel activates the Track Changes feature.

● Excel shares the workbook and indicates this by displaying [Shared] beside the workbook name.

Note: *See "Share a Workbook with Other Users" to learn more about workbook sharing.*

Is there a way to avoid having my own changes highlighted?
Yes, you can configure the workbook to show every user's changes but your own. Follow Steps **1** to **4** to open the Highlight Changes dialog box. Click the **Who** check box (☐ changes to ☑), click the **Who** ⏷, and then click **Everyone but Me**. Click **OK** to put the new setting into effect.

Can I track changes in just part of the worksheet?
Yes, you can modify this task so that Excel only tracks changes in a specific range. Follow Steps **1** to **4** to open the Highlight Changes dialog box. Click the **Where** check box (☐ changes to ☑), click inside the **Where** range box, and then select the range you want to track. Click **OK** to put the new setting into effect.

Accept or Reject Workbook Changes

After you turn on Excel's Track Changes features (see "Track Workbook Changes"), you can then accept or reject the changes that other users make to the workbook.

Track Changes enables you to see exactly which parts of the workbook others have changed and who made each of those changes. Track Changes also enables you to accept those changes that you think are useful or accurate, as well as reject those changes that are not needed or that are incorrect.

Accept or Reject Workbook Changes

1 Display the workbook you are tracking.

2 Click the **Review** tab.

3 Click **Track Changes** (📄).

4 Click **Accept/Reject Changes**.

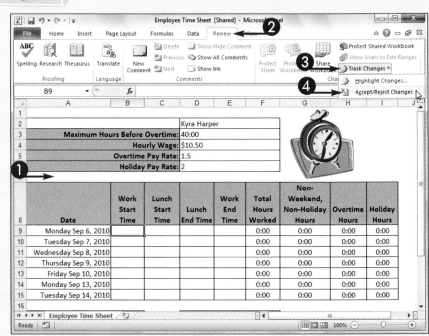

If your workbook has unsaved changes, Excel tells you it will now save the workbook.

5 Click **OK**.

The Select Changes to Accept or Reject dialog box appears.

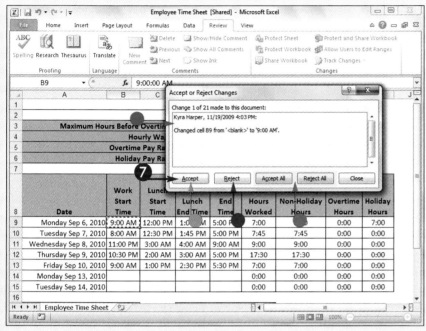

● Leave the When check box activated (☑) and leave Not yet reviewed selected in the list.

● If you only want to review changes made by a particular user, click the **Who** check box (☐ changes to ☑), click the **Who** ▾, and then click the user's name.

6 Click **OK**.

The Accept or Reject Changes dialog box appears.

● Excel displays the details of the current change.

7 Click an action for the change.

● Click **Accept** to leave the change in the workbook.

● Click **Reject** to remove the change from the workbook.

Excel displays the next change.

8 Repeat Step **7** to review all the changes.

● You can also click **Accept All** or **Reject All** to accept or reject all changes at once.

Simplify It

What happens if I and another user make changes that affect the same cell?
In this situation, when you save the workbook, Excel displays the Resolve Conflicts dialog box, which shows the change you made as well as the change the other user made. If your change is the correct one, click **Accept Mine**; otherwise, click **Accept Other**. If there are multiple conflicts, you can save time by clicking either **Accept All Mine** or **Accept All Others**.

When I complete my review, should I turn off the tracking feature?
Unless you know that other people still require access to the workbook, you should turn off the tracking feature when your review is complete. To do this, click the **Review** tab, click 🗷, and then click **Highlight Changes** to open the Highlight Changes dialog box. Click the **Track changes while editing** check box (☑ changes to ☐), and the click **OK**.

Send a Workbook as an E-Mail Attachment

If you want to send an Excel workbook to another person, you can attach the workbook to an e-mail message and send it to that person's e-mail address. The other person can then open the workbook in Excel after receiving your message.

Sharing a workbook via e-mail is useful in situations where the other user does not have

access to your network. This enables the recipient to examine the workbook, make changes to it, and then send the workbook to you via e-mail. If you want the other user to make changes, consider activating Excel's Track Changes feature, as described in "Track Workbook Changes."

Send a Workbook as an E-Mail Attachment

1 Open the workbook you want to send.

2 Click the **File** tab.

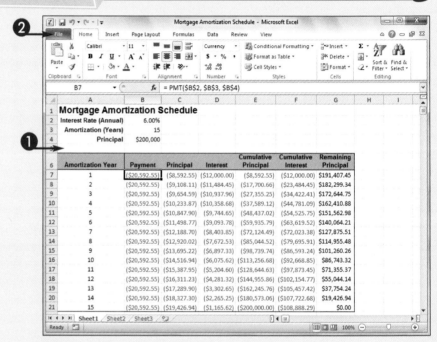

3 Click **Save & Send**.

4 Click **Send Using E-mail**.

Excel displays the Send Using E-mail commands.

5 Click **Send as Attachment**.

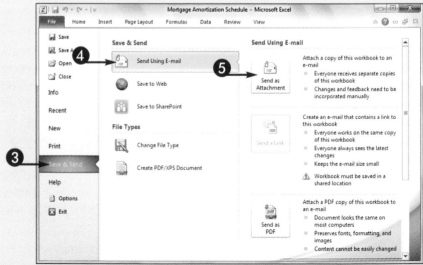

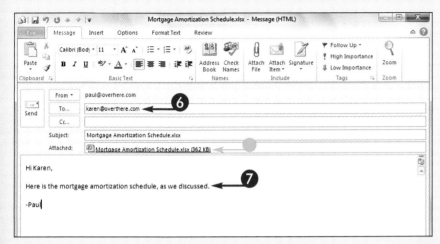

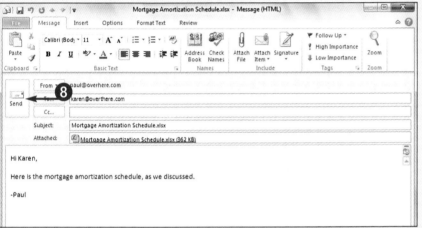

Outlook creates a new e-mail message.

Outlook attaches the workbook to the message.

6 Type the address of the recipient.

7 Type your message text.

8 Click **Send**.

Outlook sends the message.

Simplify It

Are there any restrictions related to sending file attachments?
There is no practical limit to the number of workbooks you can attach to a message. However, you should be careful with the total size of the files you send. If you or the recipient has a slow Internet connection, sending or receiving the message can take an extremely long time. Also, many Internet service providers (ISPs) place a limit on the size of a message's attachments, which is usually between 2 and 5MB.

What can I do if the recipient does not have Excel?
If the other person does not use Excel, you can send the workbook in a different format. One possibility would be to save the workbook as a Web Page (see "Save Excel Data as a Web Page"). Alternatively, if your recipient can view PDF (Portable Document Format) files, follow Steps **1** to **4** to display the Send Using E-mail options, and then click **Send as PDF**.

Save Excel Data as a Web Page

If you have an Excel range, worksheet, or workbook that you want to share on the Web, you can save that data as a Web page that you can then upload to your Web site. The other person will not be able to edit the data directly, but the user can at least examine the data and offer comments.

When you save a document as a Web page, you can also specify the title text that appears in the browser's title bar and the keywords that search engines use to index the page.

Save Excel Data as a Web Page

① Open the workbook that contains the data you want to save as a Web page.

● If you want to save a worksheet as a Web page, click the worksheet tab.

● If you want to save a range as a Web page, select the range.

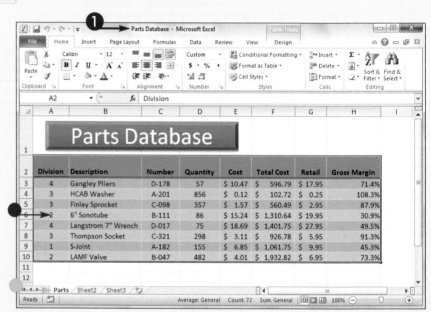

② Click **File**.

③ Click **Save As**.

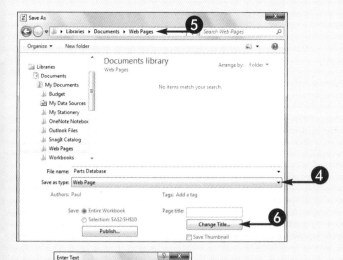

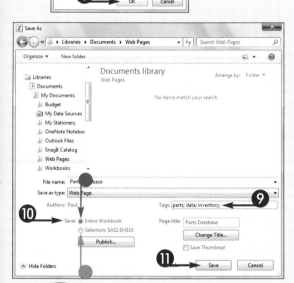

The Save As dialog box appears.

④ Click the **Save as type** ⊡ and then click **Web Page**.

⑤ Select the folder where you want to store the Web page file.

⑥ Click **Change Title**.

The Enter Text dialog box appears.

⑦ Type the page title in the **Page title** text box.

⑧ Click **OK**.

⑨ Click **Tags** and then type one or more keywords, separated by semicolons.

⑩ Choose which part of the file you want to save as a Web page (◎ changes to ◉):

● Click **Entire Workbook** to save the whole workbook.

● Click **Selection** to save either the current worksheet or the selected cells.

⑪ Click **Save**.

Simplify It

Can I save an Excel workbook to my Windows Live SkyDrive?
Yes. Follow these steps:

① Sign in to your Windows Live account.

② Open the workbook you want to share.

③ Click the **File** tab.

④ Click **Save & Send**.

⑤ Click **Save to Web**.

⑥ Click the Web folder you want to use.

⑦ Click **Save As**.

⑧ Click **Save**.

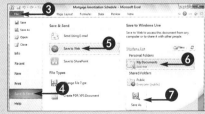

Make a Workbook Compatible with Earlier Versions of Excel

You can save an Excel workbook in a special format that makes it compatible with earlier versions of Excel. This enables you to share your workbook with other Excel users who do not have the most recent versions of the program.

If you have another computer that uses a version of Excel prior to Excel 2007, or if the people you work with use earlier Excel versions, those programs cannot read documents in the standard format used by Excel 2010 and Excel 2007.

Make a Workbook Compatible with Earlier Versions of Excel

1 Open the workbook you want to make compatible.

2 Click **File**.

3 Click **Save As**.

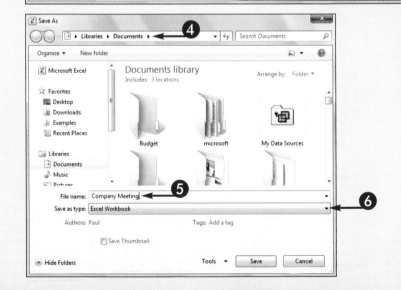

The Save As dialog box appears.

4 Select the folder in which to store the new workbook.

5 Click in the **File name** text box and type the name that you want to use for the new workbook.

6 Click the **Save as type** ⏷.

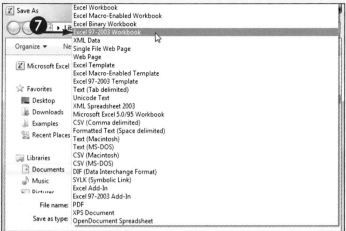

⑦ Click the **Excel 97-2003 Workbook** file format.

⑧ Click **Save**.

Excel saves the file using the Excel 97-2003 Workbook format.

Can people using Excel 2007 open my Office documents?
Yes. The file format used by both Excel 2010 and Excel 2007 is the same. If you only work with people who use either or both of these Excel versions, then you should stick with the default file format — which is called Excel Workbook — because it offers many benefits in terms of Excel features.

Which versions of Excel are compatible with the Excel 97-2003 Workbook file format?
For Windows, the Excel 97-2003 Workbook file format is compatible with Excel 97, Excel 2000, Excel XP, and Excel 2003. For the Mac, the Excel 97-2003 Workbook file format is compatible with Excel 98, Excel 2001, and Office 2004. In the unlikely event that you need to share a document with someone using either Excel 5.0 or Excel 95, use the Microsoft Excel 5.0/95 Workbook file format instead.

Collaborate on a Workbook Online

If you have a Windows Live account, you can use the SkyDrive online storage feature to store an Excel workbook in an online folder, and then allow other users to collaborate on that workbook using the Excel Web App.

To allow another person to collaborate with you on your online workbook, that person must have a Windows Live ID. If the person does not have a Windows Live ID, he or she can go to https://signup.live.com/ to register for a free account from Microsoft.

Collaborate on a Workbook Online

① Log on to your Windows Live account.

② Click **SkyDrive**.

Your Windows Live SkyDrive appears.

③ Click the folder that contains the workbooks you want to share.

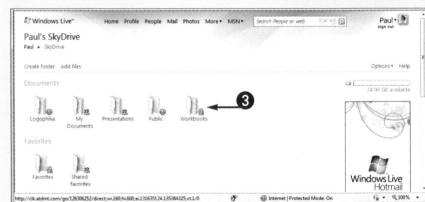

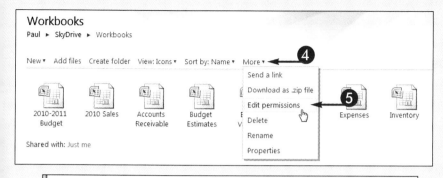

Workbooks
Paul ▸ SkyDrive ▸ Workbooks

New ▾ Add files Create folder View: Icons ▾ Sort by: Name ▾ More ▾

Send a link
Download as .zip file
Edit permissions
Delete
Rename
Properties

2010-2011 Budget | 2010 Sales | Accounts Receivable | Budget Estimates | Expenses | Inventory

Shared with: Just me

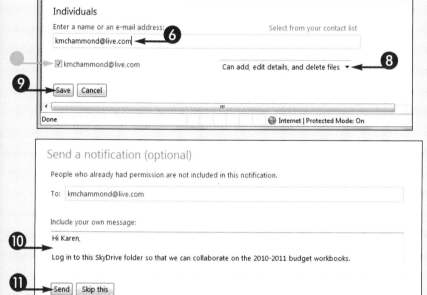

Individuals

Enter a name or an e-mail address: Select from your contact list
kmchammond@live.com

☑ kmchammond@live.com   Can add, edit details, and delete files ▾

Save Cancel

◄ _____ III _____ ►
Done   🌐 Internet | Protected Mode: On

Send a notification (optional)

People who already had permission are not included in this notification.

To: kmchammond@live.com

Include your own message:

Hi Karen,

Log in to this SkyDrive folder so that we can collaborate on the 2010-2011 budget workbooks.

Send Skip this

4 Click **More**.

5 Click **Edit permissions**.

The folder's Edit Permissions page appears.

6 Type the Windows Live e-mail address of the person you want to collaborate with.

7 Press **Tab**.

● Windows Live adds the person to the list.

8 Click ⊡ here and then click **Can add, edit details, and delete files**.

9 Click **Save**.

Windows Live prompts you to send a notification for the folder.

🔟 Type a message to the user.

⓫ Click **Send**.

Windows Live sends an e-mail message to the user. The user clicks the link in that message, logs on to Windows Live, and can then edit a workbook in the shared folder.

How do I know when other people are also using a workbook online?
When you open a workbook using the Excel Web App, examine the lower right corner of the Excel screen. If you see **1 person editing**, it means you are the only user who is working on the file. However, if you see **2 people editing**, then it means another person is collaborating on the workbook with you. To see who it is, click the **2 people editing** message (●), as shown here.

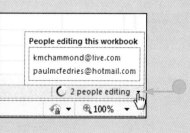

Index

Index

Index

Index

Index

Index

Read Less–Learn More®

Visual®

There's a Visual book for every learning level...

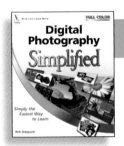

Simplified®

The place to start if you're new to computers. Full color.

- Computers
- Creating Web Pages
- Digital Photography
- Internet
- Mac OS
- Office
- Windows

Teach Yourself VISUALLY™

Get beginning to intermediate-level training in a variety of topics. Full color.

- Access
- Bridge
- Chess
- Computers
- Crocheting
- Digital Photography
- Dog training
- Dreamweaver
- Excel
- Flash
- Golf
- Guitar
- Handspinning
- HTML
- iLife
- iPhoto
- Jewelry Making & Beading
- Knitting
- Mac OS
- Office
- Photoshop
- Photoshop Elements
- Piano
- Poker
- PowerPoint
- Quilting
- Scrapbooking
- Sewing
- Windows
- Wireless Networking
- Word

Top 100 Simplified® Tips & Tricks

Tips and techniques to take your skills beyond the basics. Full color.

- Digital Photography
- eBay
- Excel
- Google
- Internet
- Mac OS
- Office
- Photoshop
- Photoshop Elements
- PowerPoint
- Windows

...all designed for visual learners—just like you!

Master VISUALLY®

Your complete visual reference. Two-color interior.

- 3ds Max
- Creating Web Pages
- Dreamweaver and Flash
- Excel
- Excel VBA Programming
- iPod and iTunes
- Mac OS
- Office
- Optimizing PC Performance
- Photoshop Elements
- QuickBooks
- Quicken
- Windows
- Windows Mobile
- Windows Server

Visual Blueprint™

Where to go for professional-level programming instruction. Two-color interior.

- Ajax
- ASP.NET 2.0
- Excel Data Analysis
- Excel Pivot Tables
- Excel Programming
- HTML
- JavaScript
- Mambo
- PHP & MySQL
- SEO
- Ubuntu Linux
- Vista Sidebar
- Visual Basic
- XML

Visual Encyclopedia™

Your A to Z reference of tools and techniques. Full color.

- Dreamweaver
- Excel
- Mac OS
- Photoshop
- Windows

Visual Quick Tips

Shortcuts, tricks, and techniques for getting more done in less time. Full color.

- Crochet
- Digital Photography
- Excel
- Internet
- iPod & iTunes
- Knitting
- Mac OS
- MySpace
- Office
- PowerPoint
- Windows
- Wireless Networking